Journey through the Old Testament

Journey through the Old Testament

Understanding the Purpose,
Themes, and Practical Implications of
Each Old Testament Book of the Bible

Justin Gatlin

THOM S. RAINER, SERIES EDITOR

TYNDALE
MOMENTUM®

A Tyndale nonfiction imprint

Visit Tyndale online at tyndale.com.

Visit Tyndale Momentum online at tyndalemomentum.com.

Tyndale, Tyndale's quill logo, *Tyndale Momentum*, and the Tyndale Momentum logo are registered trademarks of Tyndale House Ministries. Tyndale Momentum is a nonfiction imprint of Tyndale House Publishers, Carol Stream, Illinois.

Journey through the Old Testament: Understanding the Purpose, Themes, and Practical Implications of Each Old Testament Book of the Bible

Designed by Ron C. Kaufmann

For information about special discounts for bulk purchases, please contact Tyndale House Publishers at csresponse@tyndale.com, or call 1-855-277-9400.

Library of Congress Cataloging-in-Publication Data

A catalog record for this book is available from the Library of Congress.

ISBN 978-1-4964-6196-4

Printed in the United States of America

28 27 26 25 24 23 22
7   6   5   4   3   2   1

Contents

Preface

Scope and Structure of This Study

THE FIRST THIRTY-NINE books of the Bible intimidate many Christians. The long genealogies, unpronounceable names, obscure laws, and complex prophecies seem all but incomprehensible to them. Even pastors sometimes appear to treat the Old Testament as little more than a stockpile of illustrations for whatever topic they've chosen to preach, or they stick to the familiar narratives about heroes of the faith.

What a tragedy! The Old Testament is a rich resource for understanding God's truth, character, and ways. It's the Bible that Peter, Paul, John—and Jesus—had in their day. The New Testament didn't spring forth out of nothing; it has deep roots in the fertile soil of the Hebrew Scriptures. Neglecting these books or misunderstanding them invites disaster.

Scope of This Work

In a book of this size, I cannot pretend to answer every question someone might have about the Old Testament. Neither can I discuss the Old Testament without considering how it looks forward to the New Testament and the hope we have in Jesus Christ. Think of this as a field guide for the working Bible student—a handbook to help you identify important themes and features as you read the Bible text.

Each chapter has four sections. First, "The Big Picture" summarizes the main ideas of the book, the setting of its composition, and the time and places described. Second, "Digging Into" gives an outline of the book and an overview of each subdivision. Third, "Living It Out" shows some of the major theological themes of the book, designed to help you apply its truths to your life. Finally, "Questions for Review" provides some structure for reflecting on the contents of the chapter.

Structure of the Old Testament

The Old Testament includes a diverse collection of books, spanning the genres of history, poetry, wisdom literature, prophecy, and apocalypse. It typically has been arranged in one of two schemes, both of which have strengths and weaknesses. English-language Bibles follow the structure of the second-century BC Greek translation of the Old Testament, known as the Septuagint (LXX). Under this scheme, the Old Testament has five sections: Pentateuch (Genesis—Deuteronomy), History (Joshua—Esther), Poetry (Job—Song of Songs), Major Prophets (Isaiah—Daniel), and Minor Prophets (Hosea—Malachi). For this book, we will use instead the traditional Jewish order, the one Jesus probably used. It has three parts: Law (Genesis—Deuteronomy), Prophets (including the Former Prophets: Joshua, Judges, 1 Samuel—2 Kings; and the Latter Prophets: Isaiah, Jeremiah, Ezekiel, and Hosea—Malachi); and the Writings (Psalms, Job, Proverbs, Ruth, Song of Songs, Ecclesiastes, Lamentations, Esther, Daniel, Ezra, Nehemiah, and 1–2 Chronicles).

This study will spend roughly equal time on each of the three genres—Law, Prophets, and Writings. Our approach will allow us to consider each genre as a whole before delving into each section, and to reflect on presenting Jesus from each type of literature. In studying Exodus, for example, you can quickly read the chapter on the Law to orient yourself to that genre, then read the chapter on Exodus to get specifics, and then the chapter on "Jesus in the Law" to help you apply it.

As you begin your study, remember that no substitute exists for spending time in the text of the Bible itself. Think of this book as a map or tourist guide to help you find your way around. Nothing, however, can compare to walking around and experiencing it for yourself. The Bible is unique because you can always talk to the author. Saturate your time in prayer, stay close to the Word of God, and use this book as a tool to help you become the person God has made you to be, for his glory.

Introduction

The Story of the Old Testament

MANY RELIGIONS HAVE created myths that try to explain a spiritual world separate from physical reality. Stories of their gods describe how things came to be, unattached to any specific moment in history.

Israel's Scriptures do not work that way. They do not describe symbolic events or a cycle repeating forever without resolution, but instead tell a *story*—a story with a beginning, a middle, and hints of a coming end. Trying to understand the Old Testament without understanding this story is like listening to a Winston Churchill speech without knowing about the Second World War. You might understand his words, notice the clever rhetorical devices he used, and admire the strength of his oratory, but you would never really understand what he said and why. He delivered his speeches at specific moments in history, after some key events and before others. He gave them to specific people with particular needs, strengths, and weaknesses. When we understand what Churchill's speeches meant in their own time, they take on a timeless quality. The Bible is much like that. To understand its parts correctly, we must gain some sense of its chronology.

In the beginning, God created. God created physical reality as a cathedral of his glory, not as an inconvenience we need to escape. As David put it in Psalm 19:1: "The heavens proclaim the glory of God. The skies display his craftsmanship." The crown jewel of this creation was humanity, made in God's image, designed to represent him to the rest of the universe. The Lord made man from the dust of the earth below and filled him with the breath of God above. God placed him as a bridge between the two spheres of reality: reigning over the creation and worshiping the creator. The man and his wife lived in peace and plenty in a garden planted in Eden (the Hebrew word for paradise). God blessed them to be fruitful, multiply, fill the earth, govern it, and enjoy every plant as food.

God forbade them from eating the fruit of only one tree: the tree of the knowledge of good and evil. Respecting that boundary was a way of acknowledging God's right to reign. Rejecting the limit and setting themselves up as gods would cut them off from his blessing and lead to death for both them and their descendants. As we know from our imperfect world, they chose wrongly.

A serpent tempted the woman in the Garden of Eden, planting in her mind seeds of doubt about God's goodness. Would they *really* die? Was God *really* so generous? Or did he just feel threatened by the idea of mankind becoming like him? The word God had spoken at the beginning created life and order, but the serpent's words brought only death and chaos. The identity of this serpent remains unclear throughout the Old Testament, but Revelation 20:2 finally names the culprit: "the devil, Satan." Adam and Eve chose the devil's words over God's, the couple was sentenced to die, angels expelled them from the Garden, and God cursed the whole of creation.

We might expect this to end the story. The rebellious man and woman deserved immediate death. Had that occurred, of course, then I would not be alive to write this book and you would not be around to read it. God's immediate reaction to their sin, even in his judgment, was mercy. The man would struggle to bring food from the ground in a world now cursed with thorns and thistles, but he would survive. The woman would endure great pain in childbirth, but she would bring forth children, humanity would endure, and a descendant of hers would one day crush the head of the serpent. Adam named his wife Eve, the mother of all who live, confident that God would fulfill his promise. Responding to his faith, God provided the couple with a covering of animal skins, even as he exiled them. Sin has consequences, but God took the initiative to show grace to the unworthy.

Banished from the Garden, Adam and Eve began to carry out their responsibility to multiply. Their firstborn son, Cain, murdered his younger brother, Abel, and God exiled Cain. The couple's hope moved to their next son, Seth. Would he be the seed of Eve, destined to defeat the serpent? Sadly, no. Genesis 5 picks up a sad refrain, repeated over and over again: "and then he died." Adam died. Seth died. Enosh died. Kenan died. And so death reigned in a world tarnished by rebellion. Worse still, death did not solve the problem of sin. Even though every burial proclaimed its consequences, the world continued to worsen until God decided to wipe the slate clean. Noah, a man of faith and righteousness on a planet "corrupt" and "filled with violence" (Genesis 6:11), built an ark. That boat carried Noah, his family, and representatives of all the animals through a flood that destroyed everything else.

God did not need to keep Noah and these animals alive. The one who spoke the world into existence could just as easily have started again, but he didn't. He maintained a remnant of the descendants of Adam and Eve to ultimately crush the head of the serpent through Eve's child, because God never breaks his promises. God delivered Noah and his family, reformed the world, and made a solemn vow never again to destroy it with a flood. He then renewed his original promises: Noah would rule over the creation (now humans could eat meat, apparently for the first time), and he should be fruitful and multiply to fill the earth.

When Israel's pagan neighbors made a covenant—a special agreement that created a family bond between two parties—they typically asked their gods to enforce it. But Israel uniquely believed that their God chose to enter into covenant with human beings, binding himself to a special relationship with them, which he would never break.

After such a dramatic episode, how long would the world remember the lesson that sin brings death and disaster? Not long. After about five generations, humans had refused to refill the earth. They decided instead to build a tower to bring themselves fame and stability. Once again, people rejected the responsibility God had given them and chose to try to take his place. God cast down the tower of Babel, confused the people's languages, and sent them out to populate the earth—but even this judgment reflected his mercy. By dividing humanity, God advanced his plan to reconcile with humanity. Rather than dealing with all human beings at once, he called Abram (about 2140 BC) to serve as his instrument to restore humanity's role as a royal priesthood.

Abram and his wife, Sarai, had no children and no kingdom, and their names would have faded into the mists of history had God not graciously chosen them. By faith, Abram journeyed to an unfamiliar land that God promised to give to his descendants. Before, God had covenanted with all humanity, but now he dealt with a single family. The promise to Abram included the blessing of fruitfulness, a new home, and assurance that he would be a blessing to every nation on the earth. In many ways, God's covenant with Abram (eventually renamed Abraham) echoed what had existed before. But this is no case of the wheel of history spinning forever. Through Abraham, God took another step toward the revolution that would one day rescue the whole world.

But how could God keep that promise? Not only did Abraham have few descendants; he and Sarai had none at all. After many years and many more twists and turns, God changed her name to Sarah and gave the elderly couple a son named Isaac. God's special relationship would not continue with any child but Isaac. Isaac had two sons, Jacob and Esau, and God continued his special relationship with Jacob. This narrowing stopped for a time in Jacob, renamed Israel. His twelve sons became the nation spotlighted in the rest of the Old Testament.

It should not surprise us to learn that things did not go well. When the brothers became jealous of their father's favorite son, Joseph, they sold him as a slave. Traders took him to Egypt in about 1900 BC, and he lived as a slave until his master's wife falsely accused him of attempted rape. Joseph then spent several years in prison.

Does it seem like all this pain and sin hints that God's plan had gone off the rails somewhere? It hadn't; the Lord still had everything well in hand. The king of Egypt had some troubling dreams that neither he nor his servants could interpret. The royal cupbearer, formerly imprisoned alongside Joseph, told the king that Joseph had correctly interpreted his own dream and that he might help Pharaoh. Servants hurriedly brought Joseph before the king, and Joseph said that though *he* could not interpret dreams, God could. Joseph then predicted seven years of plenty followed by seven years of famine and advised the Egyptians to stockpile their resources to prepare for the difficult days to come. Joseph, the former slave and a prisoner, at that moment became the second-highest ruler in Egypt, below only the king. When the predicted famine arrived, the sons of Jacob traveled to Egypt to buy food. In God's mercy, their sin had saved their lives. They eventually reunited with Joseph, and the whole family came to live in Egypt.

Egypt, though, was not the land God had promised to Abraham, nor was it to be the family's final home. The family remained there for four hundred years while the sins of those living in the Promised Land continued to pile up. During this long wait, the Egyptians went from honoring the Israelites to enslaving them. In time, God raised up a deliverer, Moses. God revealed himself to Moses as Yahweh, customarily translated as "the Lord." Through ten miraculous signs, the Lord showed the Egyptians he was the true God and that all of their idols were merely powerless imposters. Pharaoh himself, worshiped as a god, became the focus of the climactic tenth plague, when the Israelites smeared the blood of sacrificed lambs on their doors so God's wrath would pass over them. That night every Egyptian firstborn died, from Pharaoh's house down to that of the lowest slave. And again we see the truth: Sin leads to death and chaos, while following God's word brings blessing and life.

The Lord himself led the Israelites out of Egypt, revealing his presence through a pillar of cloud by day and a pillar of fire by night. God parted the Red Sea, enabling the Israelites to walk to freedom on dry ground; but he closed the water on the Egyptian army, drowning them all. God gave Israel a great victory without them ever raising a spear. The Lord took them to Mount Sinai and made a covenant with them, summarized in the Ten Commandments. The people immediately broke these commandments, choosing to make a golden calf to worship. Again, they abandoned their proper post as God's representatives and tried to reign on their own. And once more, God faced a decision: Should he start over? Moses prayed for the Israelites and asked God to continue to use this flawed nation. God did so, leading them to the land he had promised to Abraham.

Unfortunately, once the people reached this land, they refused to go in. They feared the giants they saw in the land, convinced themselves they could not triumph, and doubted God would fulfill his promises. Both judgment and grace came in response. The generation that made this decision—everyone forty and older, except Joshua and Caleb, who knew God would keep his word—would die in the desert and never enter the land. Nevertheless, God would continue to go with Israel, provide for them, and ultimately give the land to their children. Forty years later, when another sin excluded even Moses from the land, Joshua led the people into the spot they had longed for.

During Joshua's lifetime, things went well. After he died, a series of short-term deliverers, called *judges*, led the nation. The people continued in a cycle of idolatry, judgment, repentance, and deliverance. Repeatedly, the people forgot what God had done for them and turned back to the manmade gods who could offer them no help. The last of these judges, a prophet named Samuel, appointed Israel's first two kings. In response to the people's pleas, he anointed Saul as the first king of Israel. After Saul failed, God appointed a new king, David, "a man after [the Lord's] own heart" (1 Samuel 13:14). God made a covenant with David that he would give him an eternal dynasty, protect the nation's land, and bless them with rest from their enemies. If this trio of blessing, land, and descendants sounds familiar, it should! These were the same covenant promises given to Abraham, Isaac, and Jacob.

The New Testament tells us that one particular descendant of David would fulfill these promises. Jesus, the son of a virgin, conquered the serpent, perfectly kept the terms of the Law, and as a descendant of Abraham blessed every nation. The covenant God made with David continues to advance the story line of history, bringing together through Jesus all the promised blessings and obligations.

It would not happen quickly, however. Under the reign of David's grandson, the nation tore itself apart, with ten tribes becoming the nation of Israel in the north and the two southern tribes in the south calling themselves Judah (after the predominant tribe). The Lord raised up prophets to rebuke both nations for their failure to obey the Mosaic covenant, but the people generally refused to repent. Ultimately, Assyria conquered the northern kingdom around 722 BC, while Judah fell to Babylon around 586 BC. The Babylonians captured the last ruler of David's dynasty and destroyed Jerusalem, including the Temple. It seemed sin had finally thwarted God's promises.

Even then, however, God announced seventy years of judgment, not national annihilation. In the meanwhile, various prophets continued to speak of a future restoration when God would make a new covenant with the people, not written on stone tablets but on their hearts. That covenant would bring forgiveness, fellowship with God, and peace. In this new covenant, the whole world would come to know the Lord through Israel, thus bringing to a climax the promise made to Abraham. This new covenant would fulfill all the promised blessings that came before it.

In about 538 BC, the first wave of exiles returned to Israel. Under the leadership of individuals such as Ezra, Nehemiah, and Zerubbabel, the people rebuilt the walls of Jerusalem and the Temple. This Temple, however, did not much resemble the one Solomon had built; the oldest among them wept at the sight of its vast inferiority. This world hardly looked like the last age predicted by the prophets, when the woman's seed would rise up and crush the serpent, and God would write his law on people's hearts, destroying sin forever. Judah continued to rebel, and the final prophets denounced many of the same vices the first prophets had.

And yet, the Old Testament does not end with defeat, but with a cliff-hanger. God will remember the righteous, judge the wicked, and set his people free. But first he will send Elijah to come and prepare the nation for his return. The Old Testament ends with bated breath, waiting for the coming of the Lord, who will bring about a new covenant and fulfill all his promises.

For four hundred years, the people waited for history to move forward, until it finally did in the ministry of John the Baptist. But still their eyes strained forward, hoping for the day when the King himself would reign in their midst and renew heaven and earth.

PART I

THE LAW

The Bible begins with a section called the Torah. Traditionally, *Torah* has been translated into English as "Law," which while correct is also inadequate. For us, the word *law* means a set of restrictions and the penalties for disobedience. These books certainly include that, but they also hold much more.

The first five books of the Bible contain laws, stories, poems, descriptions of ceremonies, and even calendars. Understood correctly, the Hebrew word *Torah* means "Instruction." Through it, God trains the nation how to live, including laws in the narrow sense (don't murder, make this sacrifice under these circumstances) and much more. Though few explicit laws appear in Genesis or at the beginning of Exodus, these books are still Torah. We might consider them sacred history, showing how things are and how they ought to be. Even in the books containing more explicit laws, narrative constantly interrupts to both shape and interpret the ordinances.

This legal code makes sense only in the context of a people confident that their God had revealed himself and would continue to move in history. In a way, the whole Bible is Torah; and in fact, the word sometimes means exactly that (Isaiah 1:10; John 12:34). The Pentateuch fulfills this role uniquely, however, introducing the principles and perspectives that the rest of the Bible fleshes out.

Genesis ("In the Beginning" in Hebrew), the first book of the Law, describes the creation of the world and the lives of the patriarchs Abraham, Isaac, Jacob, and Joseph. Four centuries pass between the end of Genesis and the beginning of Exodus.

Exodus ("These Are the Names" in Hebrew) describes God's deliverance of the Israelites from Egypt and God's covenant with the nation at Sinai.

Leviticus ("And He Called" in Hebrew) describes many of the practical elements of Israelite worship.

Numbers ("In the Wilderness" in Hebrew) recounts the four decades of the nation's rebellious wandering in the desert.

Deuteronomy ("These Are the Words" in Hebrew, but "Second Law" in Greek) consists of Moses' farewell to the Israelites and the reaffirmation of the covenant with the new generation that would enter the land.

Author and Date

For most of history, scholars accepted Moses as the author of the Law. Within the Old Testament itself, the Law is called "the instructions Moses had given them" (Joshua 8:32). In the New Testament (John 5:45-47; Matthew 19:7-9), Jesus affirms this understanding. A handful of passages, however, undermine a simplistic understanding of Mosaic authorship. The clearest example occurs in Deuteronomy 34:5-6: "So Moses, the servant of the LORD, died there in the land of Moab, just as the LORD had said. The LORD buried him in a valley near Beth-peor in Moab, but to this day no one knows the exact place." It seems strange that Moses would record his own funeral, and stranger still that he would say that no one knows his burial place "to this day." Clearly, the Torah has a few later editorial additions, but the biblical testimony seems plain that Moses is the primary human author of the Law.

If we take seriously the account of Moses' life in Exodus, we see he would have been uniquely qualified to write the Torah. Stephen reminds us in Acts 7:22, "Moses was taught all the wisdom of the Egyptians, and he was powerful in both speech and action." Moses' direct encounters with the Lord gave purpose to his Egyptian academic training, adding to the latter spiritual truths from God himself. And while wandering with his people in the desert for forty years, he had plenty of time to write.

The overwhelming consensus of Mosaic authorship stood until the nineteenth century, when a documentary hypothesis arose. In its basic form, this theory holds that four groups of people wrote the Law in layers, represented by the letters JEDP. These scholars generally doubt the historical reliability of the Old Testament. In their view, the Law came into existence much later than Moses' era, with each succeeding layer reflecting new developments in Jewish theology. Though a complete analysis of the documentary hypothesis lies far beyond the scope of this book, we should note that advocates of the theory disagree on which parts of the Law come from which supposed source. Their highly subjective distinctions conveniently support whichever theory of Jewish origins the author may hold. Conservative Bible students who believe an all-powerful God has revealed himself in the Scriptures have no reason to abandon the traditional view. Later contributors, perhaps

Joshua, made additions and edits, also under the inspiration of the Holy Spirit. We can affirm both the unity of the Torah and its diversity.[1]

History in the Law

If we accept Mosaic authorship, then we have eyewitness testimony for the events of Exodus 3 to the end of Deuteronomy. Since "the LORD would speak to Moses face to face, as one speaks to a friend" (Exodus 33:11), Moses could write knowledgeably about anything God told him (see also 2 Timothy 3:16). The books of the Law, of course, do not satisfy a modern historian's definition of history. Think of Genesis alone. In eleven short chapters, Moses glosses over all of human history up to Abraham. In the next thirty-nine chapters, he tells the story of Abraham up to his great-grandchildren. Genesis skips altogether the rise of the Egyptian monarchy, the development of written language, and the invention of weapons of war. Instead, it details a family squabble over which son would receive the greater inheritance. Moses shows no interest in fair and balanced reporting of world history. We might better think of him telling a theological story or preaching a sermon about how God acted for his people in and through the past. These events really occurred in space, time, and history, but Moses has little interest in satisfying our curiosity about them. Instead, through the failures and successes of those who have gone before us, he wants to teach us about God and ourselves.

Sometimes that means the Bible does not report things the way we would. It uses round numbers (compare Genesis 15:13 and Exodus 12:40). It calls places by names not used until later (compare Genesis 12:8 and Genesis 28:19). We see examples of figurative language and anthropomorphism (Exodus 15:8). We lose something vital, however, if we dismiss the Bible as ahistorical simply because it lacks the modern historical style. The reality of events portrayed in the Law lays the foundation for the rest of the Bible. The Lord did not command the Israelites to turn from idols because of some abstract idea, but because he had brought them out of Egypt (2 Kings 17:36). Isaiah rooted his trust that God would return his people to the land in the truth that nothing could be too hard for the one who stretched out the heavens (Isaiah 44:24). Because the Israelites believed their God had acted in history, they expected him to act again.

1

Genesis

The White Rabbit put on his spectacles.
"Where shall I begin, please your Majesty?" he asked.
"Begin at the beginning," the King said, very gravely,
"and go on till you come to the end: then stop."
LEWIS CARROLL
Alice's Adventures in Wonderland

The Big Picture

Moses wrote Genesis ("In the Beginning" in Hebrew) during the
Exodus (circa 1440 BC). It covers history from the creation of
heaven and earth to the death of Joseph (circa 1860 BC). This
single book surveys a longer period than the rest of the Bible
combined.

Genesis contains two basic units: Genesis 1–11 deals with
everyone on earth, while Genesis 12–50 focuses on Abraham and
his descendants. Though we cannot precisely determine the geography of the first eleven chapters, the saga of Abraham and his
descendants moves from Ur of the Chaldees (present-day Iraq)
to Haran (present-day Syria) to Canaan (present-day Israel) and
finally to Egypt. The New Testament references Genesis more than

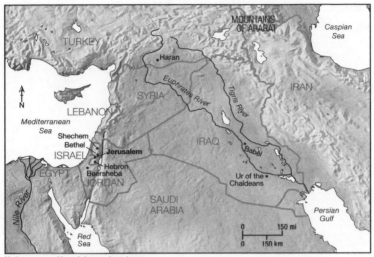

Modern names and boundaries are shown in gray.

Key Places in Genesis

two hundred times, and this first book of the Bible lays out the major themes developed in the rest of Scripture.[1]

The Bible spends little time on things that intrigue many modern people (the age of the Earth, the Fall, the Flood, and the tower of Babel). Instead, God emphasizes one man and his family—but this is not just *any* family. He highlights Abraham's descendants, who will bless the whole world. From the line of Abraham, Isaac, and Jacob, a Savior came who offers us all a new beginning (Galatians 3:16).

Digging Into Genesis

Structure

Ten uses of *tôleḏôt*—a Hebrew word rendered "the account of" in the New Living Translation and "the generations of" in older translations—organize the book of Genesis. Genesis 11:27, for example, says: "This is the account of Terah's family" before introducing the story of Terah's son, Abraham.

1. Creation (Genesis 1:1–2:3)

2. The Heavens and the Earth (Genesis 2:4–4:26)
   a. Life in Eden (Genesis 2:4-25)
   b. Fall of Humanity (Genesis 3:1-24)
   c. Consequences of the Fall (Genesis 4:1-26)

3. Descendants of Adam (Genesis 5:1–6:8)
   a. Genealogy from Adam to Noah (Genesis 5:1-32)
   b. Corruption of Noah's Society (Genesis 6:1-8)

4. Life of Noah (Genesis 6:9–9:29)
   a. Noah Rescued from the Flood (Genesis 6:9–8:22)
   b. God's Covenant with Noah (Genesis 9:1-17)
   c. Noah's Curse of Canaan (Genesis 9:18-29)

5. Descendants of Noah (Genesis 10:1–11:9)
   a. Table of Nations (Genesis 10:1-32)
   b. Tower of Babel (Genesis 11:1-9)

6. Descendants of Shem (Genesis 11:10-26)

7. Descendants of Terah (Genesis 11:27–25:11)
   a. God's Blessings on Abraham (Genesis 11:27–15:21)
   b. The Consequences of Sin in the Chosen Family (Genesis 16:1–20:18)
   c. Life of Isaac (Genesis 21:1–25:11)

From Creation to Terah (Genesis 1:1-11:26)

"In the beginning God created the heavens and the earth," Moses writes (Genesis 1:1). Moses does not explain or justify God; the Lord is simply there, ready to act according to his own will and by his own power. Unlike in many pagan myths, God fights no battle before creating, needs to defeat no enemies, and gathers no materials. God merely speaks to make the world from nothing. He creates the basic structures in the first three days (light, sea/sky, land/vegetation) and fills each of them during the next three days (sun/moon/stars, fish/birds, animals/people). Repeatedly, he declares this new creation "good."

The world God creates points to the glory of its maker. It also serves as a temple of his glory, but what is a temple without worshipers? God crowns his creation with worshipers on the sixth day, when he makes humanity in his image. Theologians debate the meaning of the "image of God." At least, the term suggests that people represent God and are made like him to worship and govern his creation. God decrees the world "very good" and rests on the seventh day.

God gives his representatives one requirement: They may "freely eat the fruit of every tree in the garden—except the tree of the knowledge of good and evil" (Genesis 2:16-17). A serpent (identified as Satan in Revelation 12:9) deceives the woman by tempting her to doubt God's goodness and choose herself instead, an idol who would be "like God." Adam, although not deceived, follows her into sin (1 Timothy 2:14). For this rebellion, God exiles the pair and curses the world they steward. Cursed, yes, but not forsaken.

God makes a promise to the woman that her son will crush the head of the serpent (Genesis 3:15). Adam believes this promise and names his wife "Eve" as the mother of all who live. God provides a covering for them, although they cannot stay in his presence anymore. Even in their grief, they have hope.

The consequences of sin spread quickly. Adam's son, Cain, murders his brother, Abel. Humanity soon grows so wicked that God determines to destroy every living thing with a flood. He warns a man of faith, Noah, and commands him to build an ark capable of rescuing Noah, his family, and representatives of every animal species. For forty days and forty nights, water rises on the earth. When it finally recedes, the survivors land in present-day Turkey, where God makes a covenant (see Living It Out below) that he will never again flood the whole world. But the problem of sin goes too deep to be resolved even by wiping the slate clean. Noah and his sons are still sinners.

The rest of the Bible describes how far God needs to go to rescue us from ourselves. After the flood, God reissues the blessing-command he had given to creation to be fruitful and multiply (Genesis 1:28; 9:1). But within a generation, the people rebel again. In the tower of Babel, they determine to make themselves a name and permanent dwelling instead of filling the earth. God topples the tower, confuses their languages, and scatters them as diverse nations across the world—but this is no final rejection of humanity. Dividing the nations is God's master strategy for uniting them.

From Abraham to Joseph (Genesis 11:27–50:26)

To rescue the world, God needs to get to the root of the problem: the human heart. To do so, he turns to a man named Abram in the ancient metropolis of Ur. God calls him to leave this place of comfort and go to a land he has never seen. Abram has nothing but God's promise that his descendants will be a great nation who will be blessed and who will bless all the families of the earth. But God's Word is enough, and he goes.

Years after their journey, Abram's wife, Sarai, has grown old but still has no child. God comes to Abram in a vision and reassures him that he and Sarai will have a son. From that son, his descendants will be as uncountable as the stars in the sky. Abram believes God, and the Lord "counted him as righteous because of his faith" (Genesis 15:6). God seals this promise with a covenant ceremony; but though most covenants involve an exchange of commitments between two parties, God completes the ceremony alone, while Abram sleeps. His irrevocable vow is unconditional. The land will be Abram's, the blessing having been secured by God himself.

As the years roll on with no fulfilled promise in sight, Sarai and Abram imagine they can acquire God's promised blessings in their own way. Abram impregnates Sarai's servant, Hagar. God rejects this approach; Sarai herself will give birth to the promised child, a miracle baby. Their lack of faith does not nullify God's faithfulness. He renames the couple Abraham and Sarah and gives them the covenant of circumcision to symbolize their unique status before him. Isaac, the promised child, is born when Sarah reaches ninety years of age. The fulfillment of the promise has begun.

But in Genesis 22:2, the promise again seems imperiled. God instructs Abraham to go to the land of Moriah and there sacrifice his son, "your only son—yes, Isaac, whom you love so much." Later, God explicitly forbids human sacrifice (Leviticus 20:2-3). But before that revelation, Abraham is ready to comply, believing the promises of God so firmly that he tells his servants, "we will come right back" (Genesis 22:5). At the pivotal moment, God speaks, stops Abraham, and provides a ram to sacrifice in Isaac's place. Of course, this story becomes even more poignant when we read the New Testament and see that God's own Son, his only son whom he loves so much, is the Lamb—but unlike Isaac, there is no substitute for him. He dies in my place, your place, Abraham and Isaac's place.

Isaac grows up, marries Rebekah (Genesis 24), and the couple has two fraternal twins: Esau and Jacob. Esau is the elder and the favorite of Isaac, but God chooses Jacob to carry on the divine promises (Genesis 25:23). Jacob certainly lives up to his name, a pun on the word *deceiver*. When the whole family believes Isaac is on his deathbed, Jacob and Rebekah hatch a scheme to trick Isaac into blessing Jacob in Esau's place (Genesis 27). Fearful of his brother's wrath, Jacob flees to the land of Paddan-aram. What a depressing turn in the narrative! God has brought Abraham to the Promised Land, and now his grandson is going backward. Jacob falls in love with a woman named Rachel and works for her scheming father for seven years, intending to marry her. But the deceiver is deceived, and instead Jacob is tricked into marrying her sister, Leah. In exchange for another seven years of labor, Jacob is allowed to marry Rachel. Between his wives and their two servants, Jacob fathers twelve sons and a daughter.

Eventually, Jacob returns to the land God has promised his family. Along the way, he encounters God at the river Jabbok; he leaves profoundly changed (but still imperfect), and receives a new name—Israel (Genesis 32). After years of enmity and separation, he reconciles with Esau and eventually makes his way home to discover that his father, Isaac, is still alive. Together with Esau, he later is able to bury Isaac in the same plot of land where Abraham, Sarah, and Rebekah were buried (Genesis 49:31).

The final section of Genesis deals with Israel's sons. Jacob's childhood did not teach him the dangers of a father's favoritism. He loves Joseph more than his other children (as a technique for remembering the order of the patriarchs, notice that their names go in alphabetical order: Abraham, Isaac, Jacob, Joseph). Israel gives Joseph an expensive robe, provoking the jealousy of his other sons. When Joseph dreams prophecies of his brothers serving him, rage overwhelms them. They sell him into Egyptian slavery and convince their father he has died.

God blesses Joseph even in Egypt. He is soon promoted to supervise other slaves, but his good fortune doesn't last. His master's wife propositions him, and when he rejects her, she falsely accuses him of attempted rape. In prison, he interprets the dreams of two of Pharaoh's servants. One of the two, the cupbearer, is released, just as Joseph predicted. The cupbearer had promised to put in a good word for Joseph with Pharaoh and secure his release, but the man forgets Joseph for another two years.

Despite it all, God remains sovereign. When the time is right, God sends Pharaoh a troubling dream that none of the royal experts can interpret. The cupbearer remembers Joseph, and Pharaoh calls him from prison to interpret the dream. The dream predicts seven years of plenty, followed by seven years of famine. Pharaoh entrusts Joseph with preparations for the coming calamity and gives him authority over everyone in the kingdom, except for himself. When the years of famine begin, as predicted, Jacob (now called Israel) and his other sons come to Egypt to buy grain. In the mystery of providence, God uses their sin to save their lives. Joseph gives us a picture of Christ, who died even for those who killed him (Luke 23:34).

Joseph reveals himself to his brothers and they reconcile. Israel and his whole family move to Egypt. Israel dies there, but his children take his body to the Promised Land. Joseph also dies in Egypt, where his body is embalmed. He knows the whole nation will one day move to inherit the land God has promised them, and so he instructs the Hebrews to take his body with them when they leave. What faith (Hebrews 11:22)!

Genesis ends on a cliff-hanger. God's promises remain true, despite the failures and sins of his people—but they also remain unrealized. Though God has blessed Joseph and provided for the family of Israel, the best is yet to come.

Living It Out

Family: The family is a key part of God's good plan for us. Adam and Eve are literally one flesh, and in marriage, God makes a husband and wife into one person (Genesis 2:24). The church, Christ's bride, is his body and shares in his righteousness and blessings (Ephesians 5:25-33). Twice, God commands people to fill the earth with offspring. This is called a blessing (Genesis 1:28; 9:1), but is also an obligation and a gift.

Sovereignty: Genesis does not describe God as one of many gods competing with other great powers. Instead, he is the all-powerful Lord of all. From the first page, where he speaks and makes the world (Psalm 33:6-9), to the last, where even the sin of Joseph's brothers accomplishes God's purposes, we cannot escape the truth that God remains in control. The same God made the world from nothing and brought children from the barren womb of Sarah. The problems of the whole world and the plight of one family both fall under his care. Romans 8:28—"And we know that God causes everything to work together for the good of those who love God and are called according to his purpose for them"—is no new doctrine for the New Testament, but an eternal truth.

Covenant: Covenants, common in the ancient world, were agreements that created a kinship relationship between two parties, with clearly defined roles and responsibilities for each. Pagan nations around Israel prayed for their gods to enforce their covenants, but the Lord did not merely witness the covenants he made with the Hebrews; he personally entered a sacred relationship with them.[2] Unlike an ancient king forming a treaty, God needed nothing from his people. He chose to have a relationship with us anyway, giving us promises purely by grace. Whether he made those promises to Noah, Abraham, or us, God's sovereignty means he can always fulfill his Word—and his holiness means that he always will.

Faith: Closely tied to the idea of covenant is faith, confidence in God's faithfulness to his covenant. Trust lies behind the scenes of Noah's long construction project but comes to the forefront in Genesis 15:6: "And Abram believed the LORD, and the LORD counted him as righteous because of his faith." Of the twelve individuals described in the "Hall of Faith" in Hebrews 11, eight come from the book of Genesis. Hebrews 11:39-40 puts it like this: "All these people earned a good reputation because of their faith, yet none of them received all that God had promised. For God had something better in mind for us, so that they would not reach perfection without us."

Questions for Review

1. How does the book of Genesis sketch out the major themes of the Bible?

2. Why does the author of Genesis draw attention to the character flaws of his central characters?

3. What conclusions can you draw from the comparative length of chapters 1-11 and 12-50?

2

Exodus

I don't want you to forget, dear brothers and sisters, about our ancestors in the wilderness long ago. All of them were guided by a cloud that moved ahead of them, and all of them walked through the sea on dry ground. In the cloud and in the sea, all of them were baptized as followers of Moses.

1 CORINTHIANS 10:1-2

The Big Picture

The events described in the book of Exodus occurred from about 1800 BC to 1445 BC. God's covenant with Israel provides the main theme. God established that covenant in the rescue from Egypt (Exodus 1–18), codified it at Mount Sinai (Exodus 19–24), and consummated it by his presence in the Tabernacle (Exodus 25–40).

Until Exodus 13, the setting is Goshen, where the Israelites had settled at the end of Genesis. Then, when Moses is forty, he flees to the territory of Midian (modern Saudi Arabia). At the age of eighty, he returns to Goshen and leads the Israelites out of Egypt. We do not know exactly where they crossed the Red Sea, but they moved southward along the Gulf of Suez to Mount Sinai. The three deserts they cross in Exodus, listed from north to south, are the Wilderness of Shur (north of Elim, Exodus 15:22); the

Wilderness of Sin (from Elim to Mount Sinai, Exodus 16:1); and the Wilderness of Sinai (south of Mount Sinai, Exodus 19:1). The Wilderness of Sin has no relation to the English word *sin*, though the people indeed sinned there. It is equally distinct from the Wilderness of Zin, located in the southern part of modern Israel, where Israel travels in the book of Numbers (Numbers 13:21).

Digging Into Exodus

The Date of the Exodus

Controversy surrounds the date of the Exodus. Some place it around 1275 BC, based on archaeological data (for example, the construction of the city of Rameses and the layers of destruction in Canaan), while others believe it was in 1446 BC. The evidence for 1446 BC comes from two biblical passages, 1 Kings 6:1 and Judges 11:26. The passage in 1 Kings describes the Exodus as taking place 480 years before the construction of Solomon's Temple, which occurred around 966 BC. Judges 11:26 assigns three hundred years between the Exodus and the time of the judge Jephthah, who lived about 1100 BC. Though the span in Judges might be a round number, it's hard to imagine two numbers from separate sources coincidentally adding up to roughly the same date.

The case against the later date for the Exodus grows even stronger if we take the New Testament into account (Acts 13:20; Galatians 3:17). Though archeology provides some challenges to accurate dating, the earlier date (1446 BC) seems more consistent with the biblical evidence.

LORD

When Moses met with God on Mount Sinai, God revealed his name to Moses. Ancient Hebrews wrote their language without vowels,

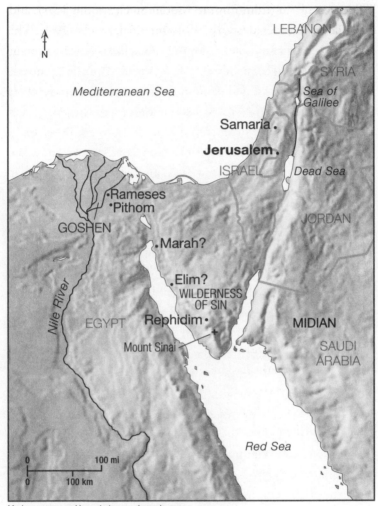

Modern names and boundaries are shown in gray.

Key Places in Exodus

and so we know only the consonants for sure: YHWH. Later rabbis, trying to avoid taking the Lord's name in vain, would pronounce the word for "Lord" (*Adonai*) when they came to YHWH in the text. When vowel indicators were added to Hebrew in later centuries, scribes wrote the vowels for *Adonai* in place of the vowels for YHWH, as a reminder to make the substitution. Eventually, this produced a misunderstanding, where readers thought "Yahovah" was the name of God. Changes in pronunciation led to the traditional term "Jehovah." Words like *hallelujah* (hallelu-JAH, praise the Lord) preserve the older pronunciation. LORD seems related to the Hebrew word for "to be," since God associates it with "I AM WHO I AM" (Exodus 3:14-16). Based on that word, most scholars today believe it should be pronounced *Yah-weh*.

Structure

Most commentators see Exodus as a book with two parts. The first half recounts the departure from Egypt, while the second half lists the legal requirements given at Sinai—a perfectly reasonable outline, but one that sometimes leaves readers wondering why these two things appear together in one book. My outline presents the book in three parts, centered around the idea of God's covenant relationship with his people.

The first section (Exodus 1–18) tells the story of the Exodus from Egypt, when God rescues Israel to be his covenant people. Everything that follows in the book stems from God's act of gracious deliverance. He does not give them the law and then rescue them only if they keep it well enough; the Lord, the God of Abraham, Isaac, and Jacob, saves them because he is faithful, and then tells them how to live in the relationship he has given them.

The second section (Exodus 19–24) provides the book's pivot, where the Israelites receive basic expectations for how they should live in this covenant.

In the final section (Exodus 25–40), God reveals one primary benefit of this covenant: his abiding presence in the Tabernacle and the Temple. The priests mediate his presence. The sin of the golden calf threatens it, but it is ultimately confirmed when the "glory of the LORD filled the Tabernacle" (Exodus 40:34).

1. Exodus from Egypt (Exodus 1–18)
   a. Oppression (Exodus 1:1–2:10)
   b. Moses' Call (Exodus 2:11–4:31)
   c. The Struggle with Pharaoh (Exodus 5:1–7:13)
   d. The First Nine Plagues (Exodus 7:14–10:29)
   e. The Tenth Plague and Passover (Exodus 11:1–13:22)
   f. Crossing the Red Sea (Exodus 14:1–15:21)
   g. Provision in the Wilderness (Exodus 15:22–18:27)

2. Encounter at Sinai (Exodus 19–24)
   a. Preparing to Meet with God (Exodus 19)
   b. The Covenant (Exodus 20–24)

3. Experiencing God's Presence (Exodus 25–40)
   a. Introduction to the Tabernacle (Exodus 25:1-9)
   a. Furniture in the Tabernacle (Exodus 25:10–27:8)
   c. The Courtyard of the Tabernacle (Exodus 27:9-19)
   d. The Lampstand in the Tabernacle (Exodus 27:20-21)
   e. The Priests (Exodus 28–29)
   f. Miscellaneous Preparations (Exodus 30–31)
   g. The Presence Threatened (Exodus 32–34)
   h. Construction of the Tabernacle (Exodus 35–40)

Exodus from Egypt (Exodus 1-18)
Substantial time has passed between the end of Genesis and the beginning of Exodus. The Pharaoh who knew and trusted Joseph is long dead. His successor begins to see the Israelites as a

threat, so he orders the execution of all newborn male Hebrews (Exodus 1:22). Would Egypt, which had delivered the Israelites from starvation, now wipe them out by genocide? No! Egypt had not delivered them in the first place; God had. He had prepared Joseph and the Pharaoh of his generation for a specific purpose. Now he will equip someone else for the challenges of the new generation.

That someone is named Moses. God used the sins of Joseph's brothers to bring his people to Egypt, and he uses the sin of Pharaoh to bring them out. When Pharaoh orders the drowning of all Hebrew baby boys in the Nile, Moses' parents instead place him in a basket to float down the river. Pharaoh's daughter finds the basket, rescues Moses, adopts him, and trains him in all the skills Egypt has to offer (Exodus 2:1-11; Acts 7:21-22). By God's providence, Moses' own mother nurses him. She undoubtedly teaches him the stories of his people and recites to him God's promises.

For forty years, Moses lives in comfort. Then he goes to visit his people and sees an Egyptian beating a Hebrew. Moses kills the Egyptian, which offers a hint of his future calling and a warning about the folly of doing things in our way and our time instead of God's. He goes into hiding for the next forty years. But even this time proves valuable; the skills Moses learns tending sheep are vital for leading the flock of Israel (Exodus 3:1; Psalm 77:20).

When Moses reaches the age of eighty, God calls to him out of a miraculous burning bush and commissions him to lead his people to freedom. God reveals his covenant name to Moses and empowers him to perform miracles to demonstrate to the Israelites that the God of their ancestors has come to save them. Ironically, Moses himself is the Israelite hardest to convince; he wants God to send someone else. The Lord allows Aaron to serve as Moses' spokesman, and the brothers go to announce the Lord's command to let his people go. Pharaoh responds, "And who is the LORD? Why should I listen to him and let Israel go? I don't know the LORD, and I will not let Israel go" (Exodus 5:2). The Lord answers the King of Egypt's question by bringing ten miraculous plagues, demonstrating his sovereignty over all the powers that Egypt worships (Exodus 7:17; 8:22; 9:29; 14:4).

The climactic final plague attacks the real false god behind all others since Genesis 3: humans. From Pharaoh's palace to the home of the lowest slave, every firstborn son, whether human or animal, dies in one night. The Lord "passes over" only the houses marked with the blood of a lamb (Exodus 12:13). Passover becomes the first feast of the Jewish year, the center of their identity as a people rescued by God's grace. Another Passover occurs about 1,500 years later, when Jesus dies on the cross. But instead of the firstborn son of the king of Egypt dying and a lamb's death sparing Israel, the world is offered forgiveness as the one and only Son of the King of kings dies as the sacrificial lamb. Through his sacrifice, Jesus frees us and judgment passes over us (John 19:14; 1 Corinthians 5:7).

In the anguish of the final plague, Pharaoh finally decides to let the Israelites leave. God personally leads the Israelites out, revealing his glory in a pillar of cloud by day and a pillar of fire by night. He takes them to the Red Sea, where they *appear* trapped. This detour is no accident or near-miss, but God's final plan to answer Pharaoh's question: "Who is the LORD?" He uses Pharaoh and his whole army to display his glory and power (Exodus 14:3-4, 16-18). God parts the sea for the Israelites to walk across on dry land, something Paul compares to baptism (1 Corinthians 10:1-2). Israel is publicly portrayed as God's people when they pass through the waters, led by God's Spirit. The crossing of the Red Sea is not just a time of victory for Israel, but a time of defeat for Egypt.

When the Egyptians try to cross as Israel did, the dry land turns to mud, and when the army cannot move, the Red Sea comes crashing down on them. This is not only a triumph of the Lord, but a public defeat of Egypt's gods (Exodus 15:1-12). Pharaoh's question ("Who is the LORD?") finally gets an answer: God is the one who speaks and controls the cosmos, who rules over the kings of the earth, before whom is no other god. And he is the one who makes faithful covenant with his people, Israel. Moses' song of triumph and praise provides a pattern for all the saints throughout history who have come to see the same kind of victory over slavery, idolatry, and death (Revelation 15:3).

Now delivered, Israel begins the journey to Sinai, where God promised Moses he would return to worship him (Exodus 3:12). If the story were not so sad, it would be funny that the Israelites begin doubting God even with the Red Sea still beside them and the miraculous pillars of fire and cloud in front of them. Three challenges arise against God's leadership and goodness before the people even get to Sinai (Exodus 15:22–18:27). But God remains gracious; he provides them with miraculous food from heaven. This bread, called *manna* (Hebrew, "What is it?"), supplies them with all they need to survive while pointing forward to a better bread from heaven that will satisfy forever (John 6:49-51).

Encounter at Sinai (Exodus 19-24)

When the nation arrives at Mount Sinai, Moses does not climb up the mountain, receive a leather-bound Bible, and then move on. Instead, the Hebrews camp at Sinai for almost a year. Moses climbs the mountain on at least eight separate occasions. On the first trip, it seems God does little more than ask the Israelites if they are ready to respond to his rescue with service. In Exodus 19:4-6, he says, "You have seen what I did to the Egyptians. You know how

I carried you on eagles' wings and brought you to myself. Now if you will obey me and keep my covenant, you will be my own special treasure from among all the peoples on earth; for all the earth belongs to me. And you will be my kingdom of priests, my holy nation."

Next, Moses goes down the mountain to get the people's agreement, before climbing up again to receive specific instructions on how the people should revere the presence of God on the mountain. The next time he climbs Sinai, the Lord instructs him to warn the people against approaching the mountain. Moses even protests (Exodus 19:23) that God has already warned them about that. But this holy and solemn moment deserves repetition. After the people purify themselves, God gives Moses ten commandments, carved on two stone tablets, each small enough to hold in one hand. Jesus later sums up the whole law as love of God and love of neighbor; the Ten Commandments fit this description nicely. The first four commandments concern our obligations to God in worship, while the final six deal with our relationships with others. Other than the fifth commandment—honoring parents, a bridge between our vertical and horizontal relationships—the commandments seem to move in descending order of severity (from idolatry to Sabbath breaking, and from murder to coveting).

Experiencing God's Presence (Exodus 25-40)

Beginning in chapter 25, God gives instructions for worship, centering around the Ark of the Covenant. Initially, this worship is to take place in the Tabernacle (the word means "tent"). Because the Tabernacle models a heavenly reality (Exodus 25:9; Hebrews 8:1-5), God's instructions must be followed exactly. Within the Tabernacle is the holy of holies, where God's presence dwells. Neighboring countries placed idols in their holy of holies, but

God instructs the Israelites to put a box there instead, the Ark of the Covenant. Within the box, they are to place the stone tablets of the Ten Commandments, and on top of it, a lid traditionally called the "mercy seat," where sins could be covered (called atonement). God's presence will descend on this ark, and his people can worship him there.

In subsequent chapters, God gives further instructions on the Tabernacle's furnishings, the clothes of the priests, the process for ordaining priests, and the holy time of the Sabbath.

In Exodus 32, the continuing presence of God with his people is put at grave risk when the Israelites, impatient with Moses' return from the mountain, have Aaron make a golden calf for them to worship. They do not intend to forsake the worship of the Lord, only to add to it (Exodus 32:4-5). Moses comes down the mountain, in a rage breaks the two tablets, and announces God's judgment upon the people. God spares them from total destruction because of Moses' intercession but threatens that he will no longer go personally with the people; he will send an angel instead. The people mourn in response, and Moses begs the Lord to go with them, or not take them any further, for "your presence among us sets your people and me apart from all other people on the earth" (Exodus 33:16). Graciously, God reveals himself to Moses and confirms the covenant with a new set of tablets to replace the ones Moses has broken.

The remainder of the book records some final details and describes the creation of the Tabernacle and its furnishings. God's presence will be with his people, as the ultimate fulfillment of his covenant with them. From the time the Israelites left Egypt, God has guided them with a pillar of cloud by day and a pillar of fire by night. The book ends with God descending on the Tabernacle in a cloud of glory (Exodus 40:34-35), at times rising from it to lead them forward, but otherwise resting in their midst. The Lord is with his people.

Living It Out

God the Rescuer: The real hero of Exodus is not Moses or Aaron, both of whom were deeply flawed. Rather, it is the Lord, who leads his people out and rescues them. During Joseph's lifetime, God used Egypt as his tool to rescue Israel. But if the people put their hope in Egypt, they would experience devastation. Aaron, as Moses' spokesman, used his staff to perform incredible miracles. Then he made a golden calf for the people, thereby failing anyone who looked to him for stability and guidance. Moses also failed, and that's why God banned him from entering the Promised Land.

And the pattern continues. The disciples of Jesus all abandoned him before his crucifixion, and Peter denied even knowing him. If we place our faith in the people God uses in our lives, whether pastor, parent, spouse, or anyone else, we will always be disappointed. Paul put it this way: "After all, who is Apollos? Who is Paul? We are only God's servants through whom you believed the Good News. Each of us did the work the Lord gave us" (1 Corinthians 3:5). God is our only rescuer (see also Psalm 20:7; Romans 1:25).

God's Presence: Moses told the Lord, "If you don't personally go with us, don't make us leave this place. . . . For your presence among us sets your people and me apart from all other people on the earth" (Exodus 33:15-16). The personal presence of God makes up a significant theme of Exodus. His presence provides guidance (Deuteronomy 1:32-33), protection (Exodus 14:20), and true worship (Exodus 40:34-35). In the New Testament, the same Spirit who led Israel in the wilderness also leads Jesus to the wilderness (Luke 4:1). Today, God's personal presence through the Holy Spirit unmistakably marks our salvation, setting us apart from all others on earth (Romans 8:9-14; Galatians 5:18). His presence protects all believers (2 Timothy 1:14), making us into living temples, both individually (1 Corinthians 6:19) and corporately (1 Peter 2:5).

Redemption: To redeem means to gain (or regain) possession of someone or something, ordinarily by paying a ransom. The term describes people freed from slavery (Exodus 6:6), the reclaiming of family property (Leviticus 25:24-28), or more abstract deliverance. Later in the Old Testament and throughout the New Testament, the redemption of God's people from Egypt serves as the model of God's rescuing work throughout history. Jesus is the ransom-price that redeems us from sin, law, and tradition (Matthew 20:28; Galatians 3:13; 1 Peter 1:18). Indeed, Luke 9:31 describes Jesus' work as a new exodus, rescuing his people through a new Passover and leading them out of bondage to a better country.

Questions for Review

1. How did God uniquely identify the Israelites as his people in Exodus 33? What identifies Christians today?

2. How did the plagues reveal the identity of the Lord?

3. What common thread unites the book of Exodus?

3

Leviticus

Take my life, and let it be
Consecrated, Lord, to Thee;
Take my moments and my days,
Let them flow in ceaseless praise.
FRANCES RIDLEY HAVERGAL
"Take My Life and Let It Be"

The Big Picture

Leviticus, named for its emphasis on the work of the priestly tribe of Levi, describes the practical details of Israel's worship. Written by Moses in approximately 1445 BC, Leviticus records the instructions God gave Moses at Mount Sinai after the Tabernacle's completion (Leviticus 1:1; 27:34). Its highly specific ordinances arise from the covenant relationship God established in the book of Exodus. God has a high standard for worship because he is present with the people, and their whole lives should point others to him. The central theme of Leviticus is holiness, or "setting apart." Believers should set God apart in their worship and should themselves be set apart for the Lord (Leviticus 19:2). God repeatedly grounds our obedience in his character: "Be holy because I am holy" (1 Peter 1:16; see also Matthew 5:48).

Solomon's Temple

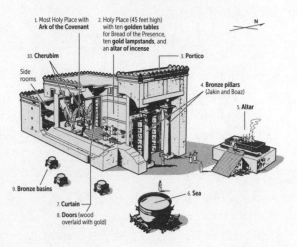

1. Most Holy Place with **Ark of the Covenant**
2. Holy Place (45 feet high) with ten **golden tables** for Bread of the Presence, ten **gold lampstands**, and an **altar of incense**
10. **Cherubim**
Side rooms
3. **Portico**
4. **Bronze pillars** (Jakin and Boaz)
5. **Altar**
9. **Bronze basins**
7. **Curtain**
8. **Doors** (wood overlaid with gold)
6. **Sea**

N

Although Solomon's Temple was built centuries later and Leviticus initially refers to the Tabernacle, the basic structure is the same.

Digging Into Leviticus

Structure

Priests have three primary roles: they *offer sacrifices* (Leviticus 1:7-8, 17; 2:8; Numbers 18:7; cf. 2 Chronicles 26:16); *help people distinguish the clean from the unclean* (Leviticus 10:10; cf. Ezekiel 22:26); and *teach God's laws* (Leviticus 10:11; Deuteronomy 17:8-11; Malachi 2:7). Leviticus deals with these three responsibilities in roughly that order. It begins with the procedures for sacrifices (Leviticus 1–7), moves to the rules for distinguishing people and things (Leviticus 8–16), and concludes with the various regulations the Israelites would need to follow (Leviticus 17–27).

1. Sacrifices (Leviticus 1–7)
   a. Instructions for People (Leviticus 1–5)
   b. Detailed Instructions (Leviticus 6–7)

2. Separation (Leviticus 8–16)
   a. Separating the Priests (Leviticus 8–10)
   b. Separating Clean Animals (Leviticus 11)
   c. Separating Physical Conditions (Leviticus 12–15)
   d. Separating Sin from the Sanctuary (Leviticus 16)

3. Practical Worship (Leviticus 17–27)
   a. Food (Leviticus 17)
   b. Relationships (Leviticus 18–20)
   c. Qualifications for Priests (Leviticus 21–22)
   d. Respecting the Holiness of God (Leviticus 23–24)
   e. Redemption Years (Leviticus 25)
   f. Blessings and Curses (Leviticus 26)
   g. Redemption and Vows (Leviticus 27)

Sacrifices (Leviticus 1-7)

Israelites make all animal sacrifices in a similar way: The offerer brings an animal to the entrance of the Tabernacle, places his hand on the animal's head, and explains to the priest why he has come. In most cases, the sacrifice must be perfect (for the exception, see Leviticus 22:23). The worshiper butchers the animal himself, except birds, and gives the pieces to the priest. The priest then takes some blood to splatter on the altar.

In a burnt offering (Leviticus 1), the whole animal is burned, so nothing is eaten. Priests present burnt offerings on behalf of the entire nation every morning and evening, in addition to those brought throughout the day. A peace offering (Leviticus 3), some-times called a fellowship offering, pictures God's communion with people and their communion with each other. The priest burns part of the offering (Leviticus 3:3-5, 9-11, 14-16), eats part (Leviticus 7:31-36), and returns the rest to the worshiper.

Sin offerings (Leviticus 4) bring purification, whether from national sin (Leviticus 4:13), personal sin (Leviticus 4:2), or other pollution (Leviticus 14:19). The guilt offering (Leviticus 5) differs from the sin offering in that it includes restitution and makes no special accommodation for the poor. The grain offering (Leviticus 2) consists of flour or cakes; priests burn part and eat the rest. All burnt offerings require a grain offering, but a grain offering can be made by itself.

Separation (Leviticus 8-16)
In chapters 8–10, God establishes the priesthood by appointing Aaron and his sons to lead the people in worship. Their ordina-tion includes offerings for their sins, preparing them to present sacrifices for the rest of the nation (compare Jesus in Hebrews 7:27-28). Chapter 11 gives procedures for distinguishing between clean animals, to be eaten or sacrificed, and unclean animals. Leviticus 12–15 describes various conditions that might make a person or thing unclean and the procedures for cleansing. "Serious skin disease" has traditionally been translated as "leprosy," but the Hebrew term can refer to several contagious skin diseases, as well as molds that form on fabric or walls.

Only on the Day of Atonement (*Yom Kippur*) can the high priest enter the Most Holy Place (literally Holy of Holies). Leviticus 16 gives detailed instructions for how the priest must purify the Most Holy Place, the Tabernacle, and the altar. The ritual centers on two goats: the scapegoat, who carries the sins of the people into the wilderness; and the sacrificial goat, whose blood purifies the mercy seat of the ark.

Practical Worship (Leviticus 17–27)

We cannot read the final, comprehensive section of Leviticus without noticing how God's holiness shapes every detail of his people's lives. Everything they say and do can worship the Lord. The Sabbath year (Leviticus 25) probably gives modern readers the biggest surprise. Every seven years, the land must go untended, leaving the people utterly dependent on God (Leviticus 25:18). After seven of these cycles, everyone reclaims their ancestral territory in the jubilee year (Leviticus 25:10). The poor receive a fresh start every generation; in this way, the Lord reminds his people that everything belongs to him.

Living It Out

Atonement and Sacrifice: The primary meaning of *atone* in the Old Testament is *cover* or *remove*, implying reconciliation. Sacrifices restored relationships with God by removing guilt. Of course, "it is not possible for the blood of bulls and goats to take away sins" (Hebrews 10:4). These offerings—acts of faith—pointed forward to the day when Jesus' death would truly make atonement once and for all (Hebrews 9:26). The sacrifices we make do not earn a relationship with God, but our good works offer sacrifices of praise (Hebrews 13:15-16).

Holiness: The law presents three classes of objects: unclean, common, and holy. The unclean were unfit for any use, and such contamination might be contagious. Common things were for everyday use, while holy things belonged to God's service alone. The Lord called Israel to be a holy nation and still calls out

Christians in the same way (Ephesians 1:4; 1 Peter 1:15-16). We must not call anyone unclean whom God has declared holy (Acts 11:9). The people could remove contamination in three ways: by water (Leviticus 15:16); by blood (Leviticus 14:7); and if all else failed, by burning (Leviticus 13:55). How interesting that God cleansed the world once by the Flood, once by the blood of Christ, and in the future by fire (1 Peter 1:2; 2 Peter 3:6-12).

Questions for Review

1. List the major sacrifices and their distinguishing characteristics.

2. We could outline Leviticus in two sections: formal worship (Leviticus 1-16) and everyday worship (Leviticus 17-27). Name the strengths and weaknesses of this approach.

3. Animals were precious in ancient Israel. Why did God make sacrifices so costly?

4

Numbers

All the world's a stage,
And all the men and women merely players;
They have their exits and their entrances.
WILLIAM SHAKESPEARE
As You Like It

The Big Picture

Numbers, fittingly called "In the Wilderness" or "In the Desert" in Hebrew, recounts the transition from the generation of Israelites who left Egypt to the generation that entered Canaan. The events described in this book take place from about 1444 BC to 1406 BC. Moses writes the book as those events occur. The English name comes from two censuses, one at Sinai (Numbers 1) and one on the plains of Moab (Numbers 26). Before the second census, we find a series of rebellions, judgments, and deaths. Of the Israelites older than forty, only Joshua and Caleb survive. After the second census, the Lord gives a series of victories, where not a single Israelite dies.

Events begin at Sinai, move to the plains of Moab, and linger without progress in the desert for forty years. Finally, the nation returns to the plains of Moab and prepares to enter and conquer the land. Theologically, Numbers shows that disobedience can delay God's blessings, but the Lord remains faithful, even when we falter.

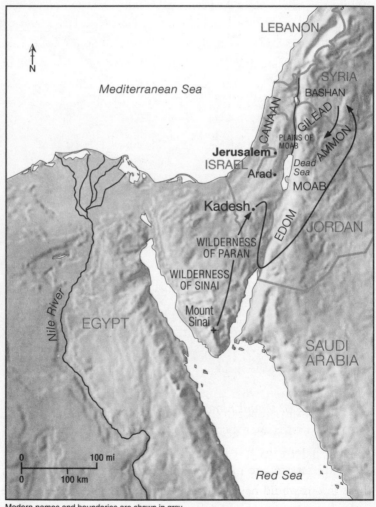

Modern names and boundaries are shown in gray.

Key Places in Numbers

Digging Into Numbers

Structure

We can outline Numbers by its three primary locations. The first section describes the preparations the people make before leaving Sinai, intending to travel straight to the land God has promised them. In the second section, the people's sin and doubt doom that generation to wander in the wilderness, homeless for the rest of their lives. Finally, when the last members of the faithless generation die, a new generation prepares to enter the land.

1. Preparations at Mount Sinai (Numbers 1:1–10:10)
   a. Census and Organization (Numbers 1–6)
   b. Preparation of the Tabernacle
      (Numbers 7:1–10:10)

2. Trials in the Wilderness (Numbers 10:11–21:35)

3. Preparations at the Entrance to the Promised Land
   (Numbers 22–36)
   a. Final Rebellion of the First Generation
      (Numbers 22–25)
   b. Census and Final Preparations (Numbers 26–36)

Preparations at Mount Sinai (Numbers 1:1–10:10)

Thirteen months after the Exodus (Numbers 1:1), God instructs Moses to count the warriors of each tribe (the Levites, set apart for God's service, are numbered separately).[1] Had they obeyed, these troops would have conquered Canaan. Israel receives some preliminary instructions, celebrates the Passover, and prepares to leave. The people march wherever and whenever the pillars of cloud and fire lead them, in an organized fashion, with the Ark of the Covenant in the middle of the procession.

Trials in the Wilderness (Numbers 10:11-21:35)

The march toward the Land of Promise is soon interrupted. Those who had crossed the Red Sea on dry land still doubt the Lord. The newly freed nation grumbles about its hardships (Numbers 11:1-3), its food (Numbers 11:4-6), its leaders (Numbers 12:1-3), and its land (Numbers 14:1-3). The final complaint, where all but two of the spies decide the people cannot conquer the land, brings the book to a screeching halt. The people are doomed to walk in circles for forty years until the current generation dies out (except for the two faithful spies, Joshua and Caleb). The next generation will take the land.

Even this does not end their sin. Korah's rebellion against Moses and Aaron ends dramatically when the earth swallows Korah, his associates, and their families (Numbers 16:32), and fire from the altar consumes some unauthorized priests (Numbers 16:35). When the people blame Moses and Aaron for their deaths, God sends a plague on Israel (Numbers 16:47-50). Ultimately, Aaron's special place is vindicated when his staff miraculously buds and grows fresh almonds (Numbers 17:6-8). Despite these rebellions, God gives the people detailed instructions for rituals to practice when they inherit the land. Sin delays God's blessings but cannot revoke them.

The next rebellion comes not from the people, but from Moses himself. He violates God's instructions for bringing water from a rock, striking it instead of speaking to it, and the Lord bans him from entering the Promised Land (Numbers 20; cf. 1 Corinthians 10:4). The people rebel again and face a plague of snakes (Numbers 21; cf. John 3:14).

Preparations at the Entrance to the Promised Land (Numbers 22-36)

In response to Israelite military victories during this period, Balak hires the prophet Balaam to curse the Israelites, but God forces him to bless Israel instead. Though Balaam cannot curse the Israelites, he can get them to bring curses on themselves by sinning (Numbers 31:16; Revelation 2:14). At Peor, the nation joins the sex cult of Baal, the chief Canaanite god (Numbers 25). A plague follows, and the rest of the old generation dies.

A second census is conducted with an entirely new population, blessed by God (Numbers 26:63-65). After a potentially divisive situation is resolved peacefully (Numbers 27:1-11), and a new leader is appointed (Numbers 27:12-23), the Israelites win a major military victory (Numbers 31) and some of the tribes can begin to partially enjoy their inheritance on the east side of the Jordan (Numbers 32–33). Jericho is in sight! Defeat lies behind them and victory beckons.

Living It Out

Death and New Life: You might have heard the expression, "It took one night to get Israel out of Egypt and forty years to get Egypt out of Israel." But in fact, only death got Egypt out of Israel. Only when the old generation had passed on could the new generation receive God's blessings. We find a similar pattern in the New Testament. As Paul wrote in Galatians 2:19-20: "So I died to the law—I stopped trying to meet all its requirements—so that I might live for God. My old self has been crucified with Christ. It is no longer I who live, but Christ lives in me." Only through death and new life can we move from sin to blessing.

Intercession: When Israel sinned, a mediator stepped in and God forgave them (Numbers 11:2, 11; 12:13; 14:17-19; 21:7). In Numbers 25:7, when Israel sinned by committing sexual immorality connected with the Baal cult, a grandson of Aaron named Phinehas "jumped up and left the assembly" to stop a blatant violation of the covenant. God blessed the whole nation because of his faithfulness. The entire sacrificial system rests on the idea that one person approaches God on behalf of another. As Christians, we have a responsibility to pray for our brothers and sisters caught in sin and to try to help them (James 5:16; Matthew 18:15-20; Jude 1:22-23). Our ultimate intercessor, however, is the perfect priest and king: Jesus (Hebrews 7:25; Romans 8:34; 1 John 2:1-2).

Leadership: Several times in Numbers, people challenge God's appointed leadership. Although Moses and Aaron both sin grievously (neither of them is allowed to enter the Promised Land), God miraculously vindicates them as his representatives. In Numbers 27:15-17, when Moses knew his time grew short, he prayed for God to give the people a new leader so they would not become like sheep without a shepherd. Centuries later, Jesus found the nation in exactly this condition—confused and helpless (Matthew 9:36). Unfaithful leaders present an ongoing problem in both the Old Testament (Ezekiel 34:2) and the New (Jude 1:8-11). Good leaders, whether in church, family, or society as a whole, follow the Lord first and recognize that their authority comes under his (1 Peter 5:4).

Questions for Review

1. List the major challenges to authority described in the book of Numbers.

2. Why does Numbers include so little information about the details of Israel's travels in the wilderness, although those travels take up most of the book's time line?

3. God does not forgive sinning Israelites until someone intercedes on their behalf (Psalm 106:23). How does intercession as described in Numbers help us understand the work of Jesus?

5

Deuteronomy

I never get tired of telling you these things,
and I do it to safeguard your faith.

PHILIPPIANS 3:1

The Big Picture

Deuteronomy, Greek for "second law," describes how the Lord renews his covenant with Israel before the people cross the Jordan River in about 1406 BC. It consists mainly of Moses' final speeches to the nation before his death and generally repeats content found earlier in the Pentateuch. Despite the nation's sins in the wilderness, God remains faithful and his promises and expectations do not change. He chooses to bless Israel as his people; now would they choose to honor him as their God? When Satan tempted Jesus in the wilderness, our Lord quoted Deuteronomy after each temptation (Matthew 4:4, 7, 10).

Digging Into Deuteronomy

Deuteronomy follows the structure of ancient suzerain-vassal treaties of the time. It begins with past acts of the king, expresses the results of the treaty, explains the terms (first general, then specific), and then calls on witnesses to the agreement. Though pagans called on their gods to witness their treaties, Israel's God makes the promises in this covenant.

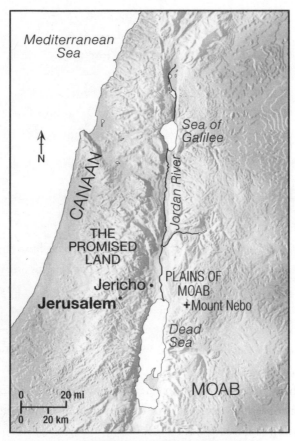

Key Places in Deuteronomy

Structure

1. The Lord's Faithfulness in the Past
   (Deuteronomy 1:1–4:40)
   a. Setting (Deuteronomy 1:1-5)
   b. History of Numbers Retold
      (Deuteronomy 1:6–3:29)
   c. Call to Faithfulness to the Faithful God
      (Deuteronomy 4:1-40)

2. The Lord's Expectations in the Present
   (Deuteronomy 4:41–26:19)
   a. Introduction (Deuteronomy 4:41-49)
   b. General Requirements (Deuteronomy 5–11)
   c. Exposition of the Ten Commandments
      (Deuteronomy 12–26)

3. The Lord's Promises for the Future (Deuteronomy 27–31)
   a. Ratification of the Covenant
      (Deuteronomy 27:1-13)
   b. Cursing for Disobedience
      (Deuteronomy 27:14-26)
   c. Blessing for Obedience (Deuteronomy 28:1-14)
   d. Cursing for Disobedience (Deuteronomy 28:15-68)
   e. Choose Life (Deuteronomy 29–31)

4. Moses' farewell (Deuteronomy 32–34)
   a. Song (Deuteronomy 32)
   b. Prophecy about the Tribes (Deuteronomy 33)
   c. Death and Burial (Deuteronomy 34)

The Lord's Faithfulness in the Past (Deuteronomy 1:1-4:40)

Moses begins the treaty by recounting everything that has happened since the nation left Sinai. What should have taken weeks took a generation, but God remains faithful. The brief history reaches its climax in 4:3, where Moses recounts the events of Baal-peor, where the last of the old generation died for their idolatry. The Lord is a faithful, living God; his people could have no fellowship with dead idols. He has demonstrated his faithfulness repeatedly, and he expects loyalty in return (Deuteronomy 4:15-19).

The Lord's Expectations in the Present (Deuteronomy 4:41-26:19)

Chapter 5 reiterates that God has not broken his promises and started over. He begins with the same Ten Commandments he gave at Sinai and then reminds the Israelites that they are his special people (Deuteronomy 4:41–11:32). All the laws hang on the Ten Commandments, but chapters 12–26 are organized around them in an obvious way, with each section of laws explaining the implications of the commandments, in order.[1] Centuries later, Jesus will argue for an even simpler summary of the Law. The greatest commandment, reflected in the first four commandments, is to love God (Deuteronomy 6:5). The second great commandment, to love your neighbor as yourself, summarizes the last six commandments (Matthew 22:34-40; Mark 12:28-34).

The Lord's Promises for the Future (Deuteronomy 27-31)

After noting the covenant terms, God explains their consequences, both positive and negative. The people are to stand on two mountains: The group on one side will announce blessings, and those on the other will recite curses. They have a clear-cut choice to turn in one direction or in the other. God will bring blessing if they obey, as surely as he will bring curses if they rebel.

Moses' Farewell (Deuteronomy 32–34)

Deuteronomy (and the Pentateuch as a whole) ends with the death of Moses. He has brought the people from Egypt to the Jordan River, but the time has come for a new leader, Joshua. God warns that the people will rebel after the death of Moses (Deuteronomy 31:14-18) and calls on Joshua to be strong and courageous. The people might not stand with their new leader, but God will (Deuteronomy 31:23). Chapters 32–33 give Moses' prophetic final song. In 34:7, we learn that when he died, "his eyesight was clear, and he was as strong as ever." We see here no fading of an old man, but the judgment of the God who loved him enough to show him the land and personally bury him, even while he was too holy to let Moses enter it (because of Moses' very public disobedience).

Living It Out

Monotheism: One of the most famous passages of Deuteronomy is the *Shema* (Deuteronomy 6:4): "Listen, O Israel! The LORD is our God, the LORD alone." Israel only rarely rejected God outright (Judges 10:6), but often tried to worship other gods alongside him. Syncretism was the ongoing sin of Israel. The Savior of Israel demands to be worshiped alone, with no other so-called deities. The Christian doctrine of the Trinity does not deny this truth but further clarifies it. Christians believe in no pantheon of three gods, but that one God exists in three eternal persons. There is no salvation in anyone but Jesus (Acts 4:12).

Sanctuary: Closely tied to the idea of monotheism is the promise that God would choose a special place for his worship. Although the Canaanites worshiped many gods at countless "high places," all these spots were to be destroyed; the Israelites were to worship God at one central sanctuary (eventually at Jerusalem). Under the New Covenant, we worship not at a high place or at a sanctuary in Jerusalem, but "in spirit and in truth" (John 4:23). (For more, see "Temple" in 1–2 Chronicles.)

Questions for Review

1. What literary format does Deuteronomy follow? How does that format inform our understanding of the book?

2. Why does Deuteronomy repeat so much information already found in Exodus and Numbers? What does this teach us about the character of God?

3. Deuteronomy does not merely indicate what will happen *if* the people fail, but how God will restore them *when* they fail (Deuteronomy 30:1-5). Why would God give the Israelites the land, knowing they had failed in the past and would do so again?

6

Jesus in the Law

WE SOMETIMES STRUGGLE to see how to present Jesus from the Law, especially in light of passages such as Romans 6:15 that seem to contrast law and grace. In fact, however, the character of Jesus and the grace of God cry out on every page. Jesus made the world (John 1:3), and Jesus promised that his disciples would reign with him "when the world is made new" (Matthew 19:28). The physical world is a good part of God's good plan, not some wicked place to escape.

Certainly, the law points out the big gap between God's plan and our experienced reality. The fall of man in Genesis, the moral failures of Abraham, Jacob, and Judah, the doubts of the Israelites in the wilderness, and the sins even of Moses and Aaron leave us longing for something more. Though many readers come to the Bible expecting to find moral exemplars, we actually find complex people with moments of both triumph and disaster. Instead of finding perfect heroes to emulate, we find sinners like us, who turn to God for mercy just as we do.

The law could never solve the root of the problem; even the first generation that received it personally from God could not live up to its demands. Unfortunately for the would-be self-righteous, Jesus escalates the requirement even further. We can't control even our behavior, but he expects us to govern our hearts (Matthew 5:21-22, 27-28, 33-48).

What is the point of these impossible standards? Paul writes, "Why, then, was the law given? It was given alongside the promise to show people their sins" (Galatians 3:19). The law shows us our need for a Savior. Jesus fulfilled the law (Luke 24:44), and "God sent him to buy freedom for us who were slaves to the law, so that he could adopt us as his very own children" (Galatians 4:5).

Election, such a prominent theme in the law, does not disappear in the New Testament but undergoes a significant change. Genesis tells of the gradual narrowing of God's action from all of humanity to the descendants of Israel, but in Christ, this gets flipped on its head. To create a new humanity, Jesus has broken down the barrier established by the law (Ephesians 2:15). After narrowing his choice from Adam to Shem to Noah to Abraham to Isaac to Jacob (and later to David), God finally brought one man into focus. Through that one man, he brings salvation to "a vast crowd, too great to count, from every nation and tribe and people and language" (Revelation 7:9).

If we see one central theme of the law, it is that the Lord is a covenant-making God. He has graciously established a relationship with his people, making solemn promises to them and offering them a chance to respond and enjoy the blessings of that relationship. "Testament" is a synonym for "covenant"; whenever we talk about the Old and New Testaments, we should remember that God has always craved a relationship with us. If we thought he went to great lengths to accomplish this by rescuing Israel from Egypt, how much further did he go when he saved us from sin by the death of Christ? God revealed his heart when he created a people, offered them a close relationship, and established expectations he *would* uphold and they *should* uphold.

PART II

THE FORMER PROPHETS

It might surprise English Bible readers to find the books from Joshua to 2 Kings called "The Former Prophets." Why would anyone group historical books with prophetic books such as Revelation or Isaiah?

In truth, our confusion stems from misunderstanding the word *prophet*. A prophet does not foretell the future so much as act as God's spokesperson. At various times, that spokesperson might announce the future, declare God's will for a situation, or offer a warning about God's pleasure or displeasure. In this way, Moses qualifies as a great prophet (Deuteronomy 18:15), though he had little to say about the distant future.

In a similar way, these core historical books do not merely contain interesting facts for interested people, but provide God's authoritative judgments on events, designed both as warning and example. While they accurately describe Israel's time in the land from entrance to exile, they always have a spiritual emphasis.

Authors and Dates

Unlike the Pentateuch, the Bible itself provides testimony about the authorship of the Former Prophets. Some rabbis attributed them to three well-known prophets (the book of Joshua to Joshua; Judges and 1–2 Samuel to Samuel; and 1–2 Kings to Jeremiah). Although the books themselves do not tell us who wrote them, we can draw some conclusions about dates from the text. **Joshua** looks like a later development of an early book, first written in the lifetime of Rahab (Joshua 6:25) but finalized at some point before David's conquest of Jerusalem (Joshua 15:63). Perhaps Joshua originally wrote the book and later editors updated it. Though **Judges** is tough to date, it must have been completed before David conquered Jerusalem (Judges 1:21) but sometime after the events described (Judges 1:26; 10:4). Since Judges frequently refers to the absence of a king in those days (Judges 17:6), a king probably ruled the land when the book took its final form. A date during Saul's reign or the beginning of David's reign therefore seems plausible. If a well-known biblical figure from this period wrote the book, Samuel seems like almost the only candidate.

First and Second Samuel must have reached their final form long after the events they describe, since the author needed to explain the word *seer*, still in use centuries later (cf. 1 Samuel 9:9; Amos 7:12).[1] And yet, if the books didn't exist until such a late date, it does not make much sense to use the word *seer* in the first place. Like the Law, these books probably were written around the time of the events described or shortly after, and later updated by divine inspiration. **First and Second Kings** are perhaps the easiest to date. First Kings 8:8 was written while the Temple still stood, but 2 Kings 25 describes the destruction of the Temple. The books must have been written during the events described; Jerusalem fell after the author began writing but before he finished.

The authors traditionally associated with these books may have written them, but even so, we must remember that God used later editors to update the language and offer historical context.

7
Joshua

By faith they, like a whirlwind's breath,
Swept on o'er ev'ry field
JOHN HENRY YATES
"Faith Is the Victory"

The Big Picture

The events described in the book of Joshua begin immediately after the end of Deuteronomy in about 1406 BC. The book connects so tightly to what came before that some commentators believe that instead of the Pentateuch (Genesis—Deuteronomy), we should talk about the Hexateuch (Genesis—Joshua). The book begins with incidents on the east side of the Jordan River across from Jericho and then spreads out over the land of Canaan. The book ends in about 1375 BC, shortly after the death of Joshua. Traditionally, Joshua himself is regarded as the principal author of the book.

Joshua, which is essentially a book of victory, is a welcome reprieve from the failures of previous generations. God's people finally begin to enjoy his blessings and drive the Canaanites out of the land. The names "Jesus" and "Joshua" are different forms of the same name. The better "Joshua" whom we serve, Jesus, brings us even greater blessings. Yet this book describes only *partial* victory. Joshua 13:13 describes just one example of many failures (Joshua 9:27; 13:1-7; 15:63; 16:10): "The Israelites failed to drive out the people of Geshur and Maacah, so they continue to live among the Israelites to this day." God fought for the Israelites, but only to the extent of their obedience.

Tribal Territories

Digging Into Joshua

Structure

The book of Joshua breaks into two parts of roughly equal length, the conquest of the land and the division of the land. Each tribe receives a set administrative territory within the nation, something like the various states of the United States. They unite in times of great crisis but have no central government until long after Joshua's death. Not coincidentally, the section of territory given to Judah, the tribe of the future King David, is described in much more detailed terms than the others. The beginning and end of the book echo Moses' ministry: The people cross a body of water on dry land at the beginning, and the dying leader gives a farewell speech at the end. The same God who guided Moses and brought the people out of Egypt continues to be with them in Canaan.

1. Taking the Land (Joshua 1–12)
   a. Preparation (Joshua 1–5)
      i. Charges to Joshua and the People (Joshua 1)
      ii. A New Generation of Spies (Joshua 2)
      iii. Crossing the Jordan (Joshua 3–4)
      iv. Sanctifying the Nation (Joshua 5)
   b. Conquest (Joshua 6–12)
      i. Fall of Jericho (Joshua 6)
      ii. Failure and Victory at Ai (Joshua 7–8)
      iii. Treaty and Defense of Gibeon
         (Joshua 9:1–10:27)
      iv. Completion of Southern Campaign
         (Joshua 10:28-43)
      v. Northern Campaign (Joshua 11)
      vi. Summary (Joshua 12)

2. Dividing the Land (Joshua 13–24)
   a. The Command to Divide the Land
      (Joshua 13:1-7)
   b. Tribes East of the Jordan River (Joshua 13:8-33)
   c. Tribes West of the Jordan River (Joshua 14–19)
   d. Special Cities (Joshua 20–21)
   e. Joshua's Farewell and Death (Joshua 22–24)

Taking the Land (Joshua 1–12)

Although the Israelites undoubtedly feel eager to cross the Jordan River and finally begin to possess the territory God has promised them, they first have some preparations to finish. God reassures Joshua that he will be with him and encourages Israel's new leader to devote himself to the Law revealed to Moses. The same Lord will lead them into the future with the same holiness and power (Joshua 1:1-9). Then Joshua issues a charge to the people, echoing God's words (Joshua 1:18). The time has come for the real test: Though God hasn't changed, has Israel? Previously, twelve spies had surveyed the land but only two had said, "Let's go at once to take the land. . . . We can certainly conquer it!" (Numbers 13:30). This time, two spies go to Jericho, the primary city in the region, and both return saying, "The LORD has given us the whole land . . . for all the people in the land are terrified of us" (Joshua 2:24). The previous generation of Israelites had feared their enemies, but now those same enemies fear Israel.

The nation marches in, preceded by priests bearing the Ark of the Covenant as the sign of God's presence. When they come to the Jordan River, then in full flood stage, God stops the water "like a wall" and allows the people to cross on dry ground (Joshua 3:13-16). What a symbol! The same God who had parted the Red Sea shows that he is still with the people by parting the Jordan

River (Joshua 4:22-23). The Israelites set up two piles of twelve stones, taken from the riverbed, as landmarks of God's faithfulness (Joshua 4:8-9). The people then circumcise all the uncircumcised Israelite men, and the whole nation celebrates Passover. This will be no human conquest, carried out in their own strength and ingenuity. God himself will fight their battles, and so they cannot proceed without getting right with him.

At last, the time comes to attack Jericho. Once again, the Ark of the LORD's Covenant goes before the people and God miraculously throws down the city's walls. Only a prostitute named Rahab, who had protected the spies (Hebrews 11:31; James 2:25), and her family are spared. Every other Canaanite in Jericho dies, and everything in the city is destroyed.

In the very next battle, however, the tiny town of Ai defeats Israel (Joshua 7). What has happened? Achan, an Israelite warrior, took some of the treasures of Jericho, which God had devoted to destruction. God would not automatically help the nation in battle. The people must obey him. After Achan's execution, the nation easily defeats Ai and sets up another stone monument over the grave of the town's king. This time, God allows the Israelites to keep the spoils (Joshua 8:27). Had Achan waited for just one more battle, he could have taken anything he wanted. But by operating in his timing instead of God's, he lost everything.

Chapter 9 records a different kind of failure. The nation fails to consult God, and as a result the Canaanites of Gibeon deceive them. The Israelites make a treaty with the Gibeonites, supposing they have come from far outside the Promised Land. Because God's people had sworn in the name of the Lord, Israel honors the treaty, despite the trickery. In fact, when enemies threaten Gibeon, the Israelites aid them. God himself aids them—he stops the sun in the sky at Joshua's request and kills more enemy soldiers with hail than the Israelites kill with their weapons (Joshua 10:11-13). Victory after victory follows, with the remaining armies of the southern coalition that had attacked Gibeon defeated first, and then the northern armies.

Dividing the Land (Joshua 13-24)

With the land substantially conquered and Joshua's life nearing its end, God instructs Joshua to divide the land. He does so (see the map at the beginning of the chapter) and designates the cities of refuge and the Levite cities scattered throughout each tribe. A civil war nearly breaks out in Joshua 22, when the western tribes believe the eastern ones have built an altar to sacrifice somewhere other than the Tabernacle. But peace returns when the eastern tribes explain they have built a memorial, not an altar (Joshua 22:34). Joshua gives his final addresses in chapters 23 and 24, strongly echoing the language of Moses' farewell address. He sets up yet another altar and then dies. Joseph, whose bones the Israelites had brought with them from Egypt, is buried in the land (Genesis 50:25; Joshua 24:32). Eleazar the priest, the son of Aaron and the last of the leaders of that generation, dies as well. Joshua 24:31 ends on an ominous note: "The people of Israel served the LORD throughout the lifetime of Joshua and of the elders who outlived him—those who had personally experienced all that the LORD had done for Israel." That generation obeyed God—but what would come next?

Living It Out

Holy War: Many Christians find much of Joshua challenging to understand, much less apply. How could the Lord, the one who is love (1 John 4:8), command the execution of men, women, and children throughout Canaan?

First, God knew the Israelites would turn to idolatry if the wicked Canaanites remained in the land. Second, the time had come for God to judge the Canaanites for their heinous sins; the Lord had explicitly told Abraham he would delay their judgment until the sins of the people would "warrant their destruction" (Genesis 15:16). Finally, the Bible calls the Canaanite cities "an offering to the LORD" (Joshua 6:17). This was no ordinary war, but an act of divine judgment with the Israelites serving as God's instrument (Romans 13:4).

Theologians have developed various ways of dealing with the ethics of the Canaanite genocide.[1] I like Meredith Kline's suggestion that the conquest provided a foretaste of the end of time, where "the ordinary ethical requirements were suspended and the ethical principles of the last judgment intruded."[2]

We should recognize that Christ did not come to set up an earthly kingdom by human military force (John 18:36). "For we are not fighting against flesh-and-blood enemies," Paul tells us in Ephesians 6:12, "but against evil rulers and authorities of the unseen world, against mighty powers in this dark world, and against evil spirits in the heavenly places." Though we do not fight with physical weapons, we should have the same commitment to offer everything to God (1 Corinthians 9:25-27; 2 Corinthians 10:5; 2 Timothy 2:3-4; Hebrews 12:1).

Memorial: The book begins and ends with monuments set up to commemorate God's acts in the past. God urges his people to remember what he has done for them because they have short memories. If they forget the evidence God has shown them, they will be tempted to wander after other gods. Joshua knew what Deuteronomy 6:4-9 taught: Humanly speaking, the faith is always one generation away from extinction. Each set of parents must teach their children about what God has done for them. In the New Testament, we have an example of this in the life of Timothy, who learned about the Lord from his grandmother and his mother (2 Timothy 1:5). We also have a similar commandment (Ephesians 6:4).

God issues his "call to remember" not only to families, but also to individuals. In the Gospels, Jesus tells individuals to share their testimony (Mark 5:19; John 4:28-30). The great commission (Matthew 28:18-20) clearly calls us to remember what God has done, both for us personally and for the whole world. Modern people need such reminders! When Jesus instituted the Lord's Supper, he said, "Do this in remembrance of me" (Luke 22:19). Baptism provides a vivid picture of being buried with Christ and being raised again (Romans 6:4). Even something as central as the good news of Jesus' death and resurrection calls for intentional, visual reminders. We should deliberately set up "memorials" in our lives, opportunities to reflect on God's work in the past so that we might tell others about him.

Rest: The New Living Translation translates two Hebrew terms in Joshua as "rest." One, *nûaḥ*, refers to the idea of settling in place. The other, *šāqaṭ*, indicates peace and stillness. Joshua introduces the concept of both. God gave the people a place to settle, where they enjoyed peace and stillness by conquering their enemies. God had promised in Exodus 33:14, "I will personally go with you, Moses, and I will give you rest." The people could have rest when they trusted that God would fight their battles for them (Joshua 1:13-15; 11:23; 21:44). They never had final or complete rest because they always had new battles to fight. But Jesus promises rest to the weary (Matthew 11:28), and Hebrews 3–4 offers rest for those who believe. We can begin to experience that rest now as we entrust our lives to God. We will fully experience that rest when we enter our heavenly homeland, prepared by God himself (Hebrews 11:16).

Questions for Review

1. Why does the book of Joshua begin and end with memorial stones (Joshua 4:6-7; 24:25-27)? What "memorial stones" do you have in your life, in the life of your family, and in the life of your church?

2. How did God make clear that he gave Israel her victories?

3. Which group of native Canaanites did the Israelites allow to remain in the land? Why?

8

Judges

The Big Picture

Judges describes the chaos of Israel between the strong leadership
of Joshua and the beginning of the monarchy. It presents a steady
cycle of decline from the death of the last elders who knew Joshua,
in about 1375 BC, to the birth of the prophet Samuel, around
1100 BC. Tradition names Samuel as the author. God raised up
temporary leaders called judges to deal with specific enemies and
lead some part of the nation for a period. They did not unify the
nation as the monarchy did later, and often more than one judge
reigned at a time. Loose allegiances and immorality characterized
the era, summed up by the refrain, "In those days Israel had no
king; all the people did whatever seemed right in their own eyes"
(Judges 17:6). Of course, Israel did have a king—the Lord (Judges
8:23). But the people refused to follow him.

The broken lines indicate modern boundaries.

Key Places in Judges

This entire period follows a pattern laid out in Judges 2:18-19. The people sin, God allows a foreign nation to oppress them, the people cry out to God, God raises up a judge to rescue the people, the judge dies, and the people fall into worse sin than before. Though the Israelites do not wander in circles like the generation from Numbers, they get equally stuck, descending further and further from where God intends them to be. Though all people sin, the judges have deep flaws. Under their rule, we see human sacrifice (Judges 11:30-40), hired priests, rape (Judges 19), and civil war (Judges 20). By the end of the period, godly Israelites long for a ruler after God's own heart (1 Samuel 13:14).

Digging Into Judges

The book begins with two introductions, a political one (Judges 1:1–2:5) and a religious one (Judges 2:6–3:6). It ends with two epilogues, the first demonstrating the spiritual collapse of the nation (Judges 17–18) and the second showing the civil war that arises from Israel's immorality (Judges 19–21). In Judges 1, the Israelites pray to God about which tribe should take the lead in attacking the Canaanites. In Judges 20, they pray to ask which tribe should take the lead in attacking the tribe of Benjamin! These bookends around the stories of the twelve judges (alternating between sets of major and minor judges) show the people's dramatic decline.

Structure

1. Prologue (Judges 1:1–3:6)
    a. Political Failure (Judges 1:1–2:5)
    b. Religious Failure (Judges 2:6–3:6)

2. Cycle of Judges (Judges 3:7–16:31)
    a. Othniel, the First Judge (Judges 3:7-11)
    b. Ehud (Judges 3:12-30)
    c. Minor Judge: Shamgar (Judges 3:31)
    d. Deborah (Judges 4–5)
    e. Gideon (Judges 6–8)
    f. Abimelech the False Judge (Judges 9)
    g. Minor Judges: Tola and Jair (Judges 10)
    h. Jephthah (Judges 11:1–12:7)
    i. Minor Judges: Ibzan, Elon, and Abdon
        (Judges 12:8-15)
    j. Samson (Judges 13–16)

3. Epilogue (Judges 17–21)
    a. Religious Collapse (Judges 17–18)
    b. Moral Collapse (Judges 19–21)

Prologue (Judges 1:1-3:6)

The two introductions in this book both give a note about Joshua's death (Judges 1:1; 2:8-10). In the first introduction, a political one, Israel asks God which tribe should take the lead in attacking the Canaanites; God selects the tribe of Judah. A resounding victory nevertheless remains incomplete. The rest of the chapter lists both successes and failures of the nation; the people conquer one place and "fail to drive out" enemies in another. For this disobedience, the Lord announces that he will not drive out the nations before them anymore but will leave some of them as a constant temptation (Judges 2:3).

The second introduction emphasizes a spiritual perspective; God judges the people because of their idolatry (Judges 2:11). God does not abandon the people, but actually fights against them

(Judges 2:15). This section describes the cycle that captures the people for generations (Judges 2:18-19) and explains that God leaves these pagan nations in the land because of Israel's idolatry (Judges 2:20-22). Together, these perspectives explain the beginnings of this dark period of Israelite history.

Cycle of Judges (Judges 3:7-16:31)

God raises up the first judge, Othniel, to rescue his people from the nation Aram-naharaim. We can see how quickly Israel falls into sin by considering the time line. Aram-naharaim oppresses Israel for eight years, and Othniel serves as a judge for forty years (Judges 3:8, 11). Othniel, Caleb's nephew, is already an adult during Joshua's lifetime (Joshua 15:17). Based on these figures, we can see that Israel's apostasy begins about twenty years after the death of Joshua.

The people commit evil in the Lord's sight once again, and the king of Moab takes control of the region. God raises up Ehud as a judge, and he stabs the king of the Moabites, losing his dagger in the king's fat. The king's servants think he is using the latrine while Ehud escapes and gathers a group of Israelites to defeat Moab. We do not know much about the judge named Shamgar, but in one line we learn that he once killed six hundred Philistines (Judges 3:31).

The next judge, the prophetess Deborah, lives during a period of oppression by the Canaanites. She summons Barak and tells him that God has appointed him to defeat the Canaanites. Barak, in fear, says he will go only if Deborah accompanies him. She agrees, but informs Barak that the honor for the victory will go to a woman instead of him. A woman named Jael assassinates the Moabite leader, driving a tent peg through his head. Since the people of that day considered pitching a tent a woman's job, her act is something like a woman killing her husband with a frying pan.[1]

The Israelites next face marauding Midianites. This time Gideon leads them, a man whom God calls a "mighty hero," even as he tries to hide from the Midianites by threshing wheat at the bottom of a winepress (Judges 6:11-12). Gideon ultimately defeats a horde of Midianites with an army that God reduces to three hundred men. God tells Gideon, "If I let all of you fight the Midianites, the Israelites will boast to me that they saved themselves by their own strength" (Judges 7:2). After Gideon's victory, the people try to make Gideon king, but he refuses, saying that God alone will be their king. Nevertheless, Gideon soon begins *acting* like a king. He marries many women, hoards gold, and makes an idol for his family to worship.

After Gideon's death, his son, Abimelech, longs to be king and has his brothers murdered. He is no judge, but rather a usurper, the tragic fruit of Gideon's sin late in life. God brings about a revolt in which Abimelech dies (Judges 9:56-57). The next minor judge, Tola, lives outside of the land God has given his tribe (Judges 10:1-2). The following judge, Jair, sets his thirty sons on thirty donkeys, pretending to be a king like Abimelech before him (Judges 10:3-5). At this point, the people not only worship other gods but quit serving the Lord entirely. God uses the Ammonites to punish them, and when they repent, he raises up Jephthah to rescue them. Jephthah commits to sacrifice the first living thing that comes through his doors if God will give him victory (Judges 11:30-31).[2] The Spirit of the Lord has already come over Jephthah, assuring his success, but he still feels the need to bribe God. When his daughter walks through the door, Jephthah laments his foolishness. By faith he rescues the people, and by a lack of faith he loses his daughter.

Three minor judges come next: Ibzan, Elon, and Abdon. Ibzan amplifies the sin of Tola, while Abdon has pretensions of kingship, like Jair. The text does not even mention the accomplishments or the failures of Elon.

Finally, the last judge of the book, Samson, comes on the scene to rescue Israel from the Philistines. From his birth, his parents set him apart as a Nazirite; prior to his conception, his mother had been unable to have children. Such auspicious beginnings prepare us for a great man, but we soon see someone used by God but enslaved to his appetites. In time, the Philistines capture Samson through his foolishness, gouging out the eyes of their enemy. He eventually destroys the Philistine temple where they had chained him, killing both himself and at least three thousand Philistines in the process.

Epilogue (Judges 17-21)

The book begins to wrap up with a man named Micah, who hires a Levite to serve in his house as his personal priest, caring for his silver idol (Judges 17). Micah expects to be blessed by the formality of having a Levite in his household (Judges 17:13). A group of Danites steals Micah's silver image and his lesser idols and offers the Levite a better deal to serve the Danites instead (Judges 18:11-21). The Danites then destroy a city to make it their own and worship the idol there for years.

The book concludes by describing the brutal rape and murder of a concubine, leading to civil war and the near destruction of Benjamin—a wildly dramatic (and dark) contrast to the end of Joshua.

Living It Out

Comprehensiveness of Sin: While the first introduction to the book considers the political dimensions of God's judgment, and the second considers the religious dimensions, Judges 3:2 offers yet another explanation: "[God] did this to teach warfare to genera-tions of Israelites who had no experience in battle." These passages do not contradict one another but give different perspectives on the same reality. From an external perspective, God judged Israel for her disobedience, especially the sin of idolatry. Yet in his sover-eignty God allowed the people's rebellion to test and teach future generations. We cannot separate the different aspects of our lives, as if we could remain faithful to God in private but follow the patterns of the world on the outside. Sin contaminates every part of our lives, but God calls us to be holy, as he is.

Kings: Judges shows many of the failures of earthly leaders and prepares the reader for a different kind of leader, marked by a love for God instead of personal ambition—perhaps someone like the shepherd Moses, or his assistant, Joshua. Fittingly, the eventual king, David, would be a shepherd (like Moses) who humbly served his predecessor (like Joshua).

In Judges, a lack of robust and godly leadership allowed the people to sink deeper and deeper into sin, but God would later use King David to bring the people both righteousness and physi-cal security. David's reign provides a foretaste of what God had in mind, but only in King Jesus can transformation occur both internally and externally.

Moral Relativism: In the period of the judges, everyone did what seemed right in their own eyes, an attitude that Proverbs 12:15 identifies as the mindset of a fool. God's standards do not change with the whims of culture. People of every generation in every place must submit their ideals to the Lord. God had instructed Joshua to stay close to the Law, not deviating to the left or right. When the next generations followed their own path instead, disaster was inevitable. Unfortunately, modern societies fall into this same ancient trap, believing they have discovered some clever new idea. But denying God's standards and substituting our own is as old as Genesis 3. The consequences also remain the same.

Questions for Review

1. Recount the cycle of Judges.

2. Despite the tremendous failures of Gideon, Barak, Samson, and Jephthah, Hebrews 11:32 lists them as exemplars of faith. What conclusions can you draw from this?

3. How do the failures of the judges prepare the people for Samuel and David?

4. The first three major judges (Othniel, Ehud, and Deborah) have no obvious character defects, but Gideon, Jephthah, and Samson gradually get worse. How does the character of leaders both reflect and shape the character of the people they lead?

9

1 and 2 Samuel

The Good News is about [God's] Son. In his earthly life
he was born into King David's family line, and he was shown
to be the Son of God when he was raised from the dead by the power
of the Holy Spirit. He is Jesus Christ our Lord.

ROMANS 1:3-4

The Big Picture

Originally one book (later divided by the translators of the Septuagint), 1 and 2 Samuel describe the rise of the united Hebrew monarchy from the prophet Samuel through the reigns of Saul and David. The narrative highlights the relocation of the Ark of the Covenant to Jerusalem, uniting the spiritual and political centers of the nation. It treats both Saul and David with frank honesty, describing in detail their failures and their strengths. Samuel includes very few theological assessments of the events, preferring simply to describe the history and let the reader evaluate them based on the Law (especially Deuteronomy).

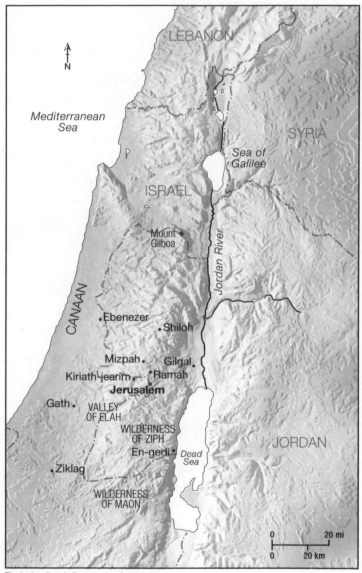

The broken lines indicate modern boundaries.

Key Places in 1 and 2 Samuel

Digging Into 1 and 2 Samuel

Structure

1. End of the Judges (1 Samuel 1–7)
   a. Samuel's Birth and Calling (1 Samuel 1–3)
   b. The Ark (1 Samuel 4–7)

2. Reign of Saul (1 Samuel 8–15)
   a. The Rise of Saul (1 Samuel 8–12)
   b. The Fall of Saul (1 Samuel 13–15)

3. Rise of David (1 Samuel 16—2 Samuel 4)
   a. David's Preparation (1 Samuel 16–27)
   b. The Death of Saul (1 Samuel 28–31)
   c. David's Unification of Israel (2 Samuel 1–4)

4. Reign of David (2 Samuel 5–24)
   a. David's Consolidation of His Territory
      (2 Samuel 5–6)
   b. The Davidic Covenant (2 Samuel 7)
   c. The Strength of David's Reign (2 Samuel 8–10)
   d. David's Sin with Bathsheba (2 Samuel 11–12)
   e. Internal Threats to David's Reign (2 Samuel 13–20)
   f. David's Death (2 Samuel 21–24)

End of the Judges (1 Samuel 1-7)

By the end of the book of Judges, the nation has plunged into political and religious turmoil. The behavior of the Levites, the ones entrusted with defending God's Law, makes clear that everyone in the time of the judges does whatever seems right in their own eyes. During this dark period, a woman comes to the Tabernacle to pour out her heart to God because of her barren womb. She promises that if God will give her a son, she will devote him to Temple service. God allows her to become pregnant, and her son, Samuel, is set apart from birth, like Samson before him.

Samuel chooses to live in obedience and serves Eli the priest in the Temple from a young age. Eli's own sons choose a very different path, using the priesthood as a means of personal gain. God calls Samuel out as a prophet when he is still a child and entrusts him with a message of inevitable judgment on Eli's house (1 Samuel 3:11-14).

At the same time, Israel again goes to war with the Philistines and suffers a humiliating defeat.[1] The Israelites believe the mere presence of the Ark will obligate God to fight for them. They forget that Joshua had prepared the people first, before taking the Ark into battle. This time, with the Ark a mere empty symbol going before a rebellious nation, they suffer more than *seven times* as many losses as they had without it (1 Samuel 4:2, 10). The Philistines kill Eli's two sons and capture the Ark. When Eli hears the news, the obese ninety-eight-year-old falls backward in shock, breaks his neck, and dies. After a delightful display of the Lord's supremacy over the Philistine god Dagon (1 Samuel 5:1–7:4), the Ark returns to Israel.

When Samuel grows up, he calls the people to repent of their idolatry and turn back to God. They tear down their idols, Samuel intercedes on their behalf, and God gives them victory. Samuel's sphere of influence seems to grow broader than that of most previous judges, and he travels in a circuit to guide the people (1 Samuel 7:15-17).

Reign of Saul (1 Samuel 8-15)

When Samuel grows old and his sons appear as unfit for leadership as Eli's had been, the people demand a king. The Lord tells Samuel to give them a king, but first he must warn them about the consequences of behaving like the nations rather than allowing God to reign over them. Nevertheless, they want "to be like the nations around [them]" (1 Samuel 8:20). God appoints Saul as king. His introduction is more interesting for what it does not say than for what it does. The text describes Saul as tall and handsome but says nothing about his character. The Spirit of the Lord descends upon Saul, who defeats the Ammonites (1 Samuel 11).

Sadly, the first king of Israel falls into the same error as the judges before him: He does what seems right in his own eyes. Although God honors him as king and allows him to prophesy (1 Samuel 10:10), Saul presumptuously offers a sacrifice as a priest (1 Samuel 13:8-11). For this rebellion, God puts an end to Saul's dynasty and replaces him with "a man after his own heart" (1 Samuel 13:14). Rather than repenting, Saul once again takes his own path instead of God's, thus sealing his own rejection (1 Samuel 15:20-23).

Rise of David (1 Samuel 16–2 Samuel 4)

God sends Samuel to anoint the new king of Israel by smearing olive oil on his head as a symbol of God's Spirit. Samuel expects someone who looks like a king, but God warns him, "Don't judge by his appearance or height. . . . People judge by outward appearance, but the LORD looks at the heart" (1 Samuel 16:7). The young man whom God selects, the youngest son of Jesse, lives in the little village of Bethlehem, and a strange situation follows. Samuel anoints David and God's Spirit comes on him, but Saul still sits on the throne of Israel. Compare this delay to our own era, the time between the ascension of Jesus and his return. Jesus is truly the King, even though his Kingdom has not yet been fully revealed (Hebrews 2:9).

During this preparation phase, God allows David to play the harp in Saul's palace and serve as his beloved armor-bearer (1 Samuel 16:18-21). David travels back and forth between Saul's court and Bethlehem, still caring for his father's sheep. Then comes one of the best-known stories of the Bible. Goliath, a giant from the city of Gath, leads the Philistine forces to the valley of Elah and challenges the Israelites to representative combat (1 Samuel 17). All the Israelites are afraid to battle with this giant, a seasoned warrior about nine feet nine inches (three meters) tall. For forty days, Goliath taunts the nation and blasphemes the Lord. Only David, not yet twenty years old (compare 1 Samuel 17:33 with Numbers 1:3), dares to stand up to him. God uses David's faith to stand in as Israel's representative and rescue the nation, a stunning foreshadowing of the covenant to follow in 2 Samuel 7.

After this victory, Saul's love for David turns to jealousy. He wants information on David's family to determine whether they might become potential political rivals (1 Samuel 17:55-58; 18:6-9). For the rest of his life, Saul languishes in jealousy and pride. He tries to kill David (1 Samuel 18:10-11; 19:9-10) and have him killed (1 Samuel 18:25; 19:1, 11-15), so David must hide. In his mad pursuit, Saul slaughters priests and uses foreigners as his spies (1 Samuel 22), while David fights Israel's enemies, the proper role of the king (1 Samuel 23, 27, 30). David also twice spares Saul's life out of respect for the king, "the LORD's anointed one" (1 Samuel 24, 26). At last, God uses the Philistine army to kill Saul and three of his sons (1 Samuel 31). The enemies Saul had failed to defeat finally ensnare him. Over the next seven and a half years, David reigns over Judah until Saul's remaining son (Ishbosheth) dies.

Reign of David (2 Samuel 5-24)

Once Saul's final heir dies, David unifies all twelve tribes and conquers Jerusalem, making it his capital. Then he drives the Philistines out of Israel's territory, accomplishing the work that both Saul and Samson had left undone (2 Samuel 5). He moves the Ark of the Covenant to Jerusalem, uniting the political and spiritual centers of the nation (2 Samuel 6). David asks the prophet Nathan for permission to build a temple for the Lord (2 Samuel 7), but God forbids him from doing so. Instead, God says he will build David a house (that is, a lasting lineage). Second Samuel 8–10 describe some of David's victories, but his sin endangers his work (2 Samuel 11). The king sees a beautiful woman, Bathsheba, taking a bath, and he calls her to the palace. Will David, who had defeated the Philistines—something that eluded Samson—fall into the same snare that ruined Samson? Bathsheba becomes pregnant, and David has her husband, Uriah, killed to cover up his sin. But when Nathan the prophet confronts the guilty king with a powerful parable, David repents and writes the famous Psalm 51.

David and Bathsheba's first child dies (2 Samuel 12:23 gives us a powerful picture of hope in the face of death), but she becomes pregnant again. They name this child Solomon, and he is destined to become David's heir and the ancestor of Jesus. But the effects of sin linger, and David's family soon falls into pieces. His son Amnon rapes his half-sister Tamar (2 Samuel 13:1-22). When David does nothing about it, his other son, Absalom, kills Amnon (2 Samuel 13:23-33). Again, David does not discipline his son, and eventually Absalom leads a rebellion against David (2 Samuel 15–17). Joab, David's general, murders Absalom (2 Samuel 18:14). In the final chapter (2 Samuel 24), David orders a census that prompts God to send a plague on the nation. God stops the plague just short of Jerusalem, on a flat hilltop called a threshing floor. David purchases that spot to build an altar, which later becomes the site of the Temple (2 Chronicles 3:1). It's not the last time God will suspend his justice in favor of his mercy.

Living It Out

Davidic Covenant: The Davidic covenant is spelled out in 2 Samuel 7, one of the key chapters in the Bible. David wanted to build God a house, but in a wordplay, God declared that he would build David a house instead—an eternal family. In this section, God takes many of the promises previously tied to the obedience of Israel and narrows them to David's descendants. We see here the same basic elements of Genesis 12:1-7: God will give him a great name, descendants, and the land. How beautiful for us, because we know God will narrow it even further. One everlasting King, perfect in obedience, will one day bring blessing to the whole world. Jesus, the Son of David, perfectly and ultimately fulfills God's promise to David. Even more, though David wanted to build a temple where God could dwell, the fullness of God will ultimately dwell in David's heir (Colossians 2:9).

Parenthood: Eli, Samuel, and David, all righteous men in their personal lives, brought heartbreak on everyone around them by indulging their children. Eli's permissiveness with his sons meant that he honored his children more than God (1 Samuel 2:29). The wickedness of Samuel's sons prompted the people to demand a king (1 Samuel 8:5). David's refusal to deal with the aftermath of Tamar's rape led to chaos and his temporary exile from Jerusalem. All three men failed to remember the fundamental commandment to pass along God's truth to their children (Deuteronomy 6:4-8). Note that Eli and David did their children no favors by being too soft on their sin. Because they did not raise their children "with the discipline and instruction that comes from the Lord" (Ephesians 6:4), the Lord judged their children instead.

Questions for Review

1. How did Samuel help Israel transition from the time of the judges to the monarchy?

2. Why does David's sin with Bathsheba take up so much space in this narrative?

3. Compare and contrast David and Saul. Why did the people want Saul as their king? Why did God want David to become king?

4. List some similarities between Samuel and John the Baptist. Why do you think God chose to use men with similar characteristics to play comparable roles?

10

1 and 2 Kings

This is the property of that eternal and just law of God, that he who would not be ruled with gentleness by God, should be ruled as a punishment by his own self; and that all those who have willingly thrown off the gentle yoke and light burden of charity should bear unwillingly the insupportable burden of their own will.

BERNARD OF CLAIRVAUX

The Big Picture

Where 1–2 Samuel describes the gradual ascent of the Hebrew monarchy from the end of the judges to the height of King David's power, 1–2 Kings tells of the nation's decline and fall. The events begin about 970 BC with the death of David and the ascent of his son Solomon to the throne. Solomon, a powerful leader, undermines his wisdom by marrying many idolaters. His son Rehoboam provokes the northern tribes to rebellion. Jeroboam I, the rebellion's leader, becomes king of the northern tribes (Israel) and sets a pattern of wickedness and idolatry that continues until the Assyrians destroy the nation in 722 BC. During that time, God sends prophets—Elijah, Elisha, and Isaiah—to call the people back, but to no avail. Meanwhile, the two southern tribes (Judah) have a few righteous kings scattered among many wicked ones. In 586 BC, Babylonian forces destroy both Jerusalem and the Temple, slaughtering or exiling most of God's people.

The broken lines indicate modern boundaries.

Key Places in 1 and 2 Kings

Digging Into 1 and 2 Kings

Structure

Three falls provide the outline for 1 and 2 Kings. Shortly after Solomon's death, the united monarchy falls. After a stream of wicked rulers, the northern nation of Israel falls to Assyria. Despite a few sparks of hope, Judah eventually falls to the Babylonians.

1. The United Monarchy (1 Kings 1:1–14:20)
   a. Reaching the Throne (1 Kings 1–2)
   b. Wisdom (1 Kings 3–4)
   c. Building the Temple (1 Kings 5–9)
   d. Solomon's Pride (1 Kings 10–11)
   e. The United Kingdom's Fall to Jeroboam
      (1 Kings 12:1–14:20)

2. Israel and Judah Divided (1 Kings 14:21—2 Kings 17:41)
   a. Rehoboam, Abijah, and Asa of Judah
      (1 Kings 14:21–15:24)
   b. Nadab, Baasha, Elah, Zimri, and Omri of Israel
      (1 Kings 15:25–16:28)
   c. Elijah's Ministry [Jehoshaphat of Judah; Ahab and Ahaziah of Israel] (1 Kings 16:29—2 Kings 2:12)
   d. Elisha's Ministry [Jeroboam of Israel; Jehoram and Ahaziah of Judah] (2 Kings 2:13–8:29)
   e. Jehu of Israel; Joash of Judah (2 Kings 9–12)
   f. Jehoahaz, Jehoash, Jeroboam II, and Zechariah of Israel and Amaziah, Uzziah of Judah
      (2 Kings 13:1–15:12)

g. Shallum, Menahem, Pekahiah, Pekah, and
   Hoshea of Israel; Jotham and Ahaz of Judah
   (2 Kings 15:13–17:4)
h. The Fall of Israel to Assyria (2 Kings 17:5-41)

3. Judah Alone (2 Kings 18–25)
   a. Righteous Hezekiah, wicked Manasseh, and Amon
      (2 Kings 18–21)
   b. Righteous Josiah, wicked Jehoahaz, Jehoiakim,
      Zedekiah (2 Kings 22–24)
   c. The Fall of Judah to Babylon (2 Kings 25)

The United Monarchy (1 Kings 1:1-14:20)

First Kings picks up immediately after the end of 2 Samuel, follow-ing David's reign. David's failure to properly raise his own family causes another round of pain for him when his eldest son, Adonijah, begins behaving like a king while David yet lives (1 Kings 1:5-6). Nathan the prophet, God's instrument for challenging David's sin with Bathsheba, helps bring Solomon to power. While Nathan remains loyal to God first, his love for the king fuels his support of Solomon. By contrast, Joab, the ruthless soldier selected as David's commander, sides with Adonijah.

Once Solomon ascends to the throne, God comes to him in a vision and offers to give him whatever he wants. Solomon asks for the wisdom to carry out God's will, and for this wise choice the Lord blesses him and gives him all that he did not request (1 Kings 3:10-14). Solomon's crowning achievement is the construction of the Temple using a conscripted labor force of thirty thou-sand men. Construction begins 480 years after the exodus from Egypt—twelve generations of forty years each (1 Kings 6:1)—and takes seven years to complete (1 Kings 6:38). Though not large by ancient standards (only ninety feet long by thirty feet wide; see the illustration in the chapter on Leviticus for a diagram), the Temple's craftsmanship is of the highest quality imaginable. Cherubim and garden imagery decorate the Temple, like the Tabernacle before it. Also like the Tabernacle, when priests place the Ark of the Covenant in the center of the completed Temple, God's presence descends visibly. Solomon sacrifices hundreds of thousands of animals in praise (1 Kings 8:62-63 describes almost 150,000 animal sacrifices from Solomon alone).

After Solomon's prayer of dedication, the Lord comes to Solomon in another vision, reaffirming his promises to David but warning that the presence of the Temple will not prevent God from judging the people if they turn away from him (1 Kings 9:1-9). Solomon does not quite get the picture. He marries the daughter of Pharaoh (1 Kings 9:16) and eventually marries seven hundred women and takes three hundred others as concubines. The foreign gods of these women draw him away from the Lord, and he worships even Chemosh and Molech, whose cults include human sacrifice (1 Kings 11:1-8). For his sins, God announces that he will divide the kingdom after Solomon's death, leaving David's immediate heirs to rule over Judah and Benjamin alone (1 Kings 11:9-13, 39).

During Solomon's lifetime, God promises to give Jeroboam the throne of the ten northern tribes and assures him that, if he is faithful, God will give him a lasting dynasty (1 Kings 11:29-39). Jeroboam flees the country until Rehoboam becomes king after the death of his father, Solomon. Rehoboam alienates the northern tribes by unnecessarily burdening them, allowing Jeroboam to take control. The Lord sends a prophet who narrowly stops a civil war, but the nation has decisively ruptured (1 Kings 12:21-24).

Jeroboam sets up the capital of Israel in Shechem. Fearing

that if the Israelites continue to visit the Temple in Jerusalem they will return to Judah, he sets up golden calves in Bethel and Dan. Remarkably, he repeats the language Aaron had used over the first golden calf in Exodus 32:4. Throughout his life, Jeroboam leads the new nation of Israel into idolatry. Jeroboam's name becomes a proverb for wickedness (1 Kings 15:34; 16:31; 22:52; 2 Kings 3:3; 10:31; 13:6; 15:28), and the nation follows the trajectory he set, to its downfall. As a mnemonic help, notice that the two nations appear in alphabetical order, with Israel north of Judah. Israel gets to keep the country's name, while Judah keeps the capital (Jerusalem).

Israel and Judah Divided (1 Kings 14:21–2 Kings 17:41)

The next several kings of Israel continue the nation's descent into the madness of idolatry, and all have unstable dynasties. Omri takes the throne after his predecessor's reign of only seven days (1 Kings 16:15). We remember Omri for two reasons. First, he moves the capital of Israel to Samaria, where it remains for the rest of the nation's existence (1 Kings 16:21-28). Second, he surpasses all of his predecessors in wickedness. But his infamy lasts only a single generation, until his son, Ahab, takes his place (1 Kings 16:25, 30).

Ahab rules over Israel during the ministries of the great prophets Elijah and Elisha. Although a three-year drought at the Lord's command demonstrates the impotence of the Canaanite storm god Baal, Ahab and his wife, Jezebel, continue to worship both Baal and the goddess Asherah.[1] The most memorable moment of Elijah's ministry comes in a dramatic confrontation on Mount Carmel, when the Lord sends fire to consume a sacrifice, thus revealing himself as the true and living God. After that, God reveals himself to Elijah on Mount Sinai (Horeb) and explains that the prophet has nearly completed his ministry. He will anoint Elisha as the next prophet, Jehu as the next king of Israel, and Hazael as the king of Aram (who will take control of Israel when Jehu is unfaithful to the Lord). In the meantime, God gives Ahab a chance to prove himself faithful when he gives Israel victory against Ben-hadad, but Ahab walks in the steps of Saul and frees the man God said should die, sealing his own fate (1 Kings 20).

In 2 Kings 2, Elijah parts the Jordan River with his cloak and is taken up to heaven in a whirlwind. Elisha, Elijah's successor, parts the Jordan River again on his way back across and performs many of the same miracles as Elijah (2 Kings 2, 4), although he performs twice as many as his mentor. The same Lord is with Elisha who was with Elijah, Joshua, and Moses. Second Kings 5 recounts Elisha's healing of Namaan, the Gentile leper, who washes in the Jordan River seven times. Second Kings 6–7 shows God's gracious deliverance of Israel despite the nation's wickedness. In chapters 9–10, Jezebel and the rest of Ahab's line are killed, but the nation continues in sin.

Israel quickly collapses, as the Assyrians destroy the nation and carry most of its survivors into exile (2 Kings 15–17). The first wave of destruction (733 BC–732 BC), under Tiglath-pileser III, removes the best of the land (as the Babylonian king, Nebuchadnezzar, would later do with Daniel and his three companions). The second wave (722 BC–721 BC), under Shalmaneser V, finishes the job. Second Kings 17:24-29 describes widespread intermarriage between pagan immigrants and the poorest Israelites, who had been allowed to remain in the land, resulting in religious syncretism. This ungodly mixing ultimately would lead to the group known in the Gospels as the Samaritans.

Judah Alone (2 Kings 18–25)

Though Israel has no good kings, Judah has several. Asa (1 Kings 15), Jehoshaphat (1 Kings 22), Joash (2 Kings 11–12), Amaziah (2 Kings 14), Uzziah (2 Kings 15), and Jotham (2 Kings 15) all are relatively righteous. After the fall of Israel, Judah has only two more good kings.

The first, Hezekiah (2 Kings 18–20), successfully breaks the dominance of Assyria over Judah, stops the worship of idols, and is "successful in everything he did" (2 Kings 18:7). Sennacherib, the king of Assyria, threatens Judah, but the prophet Isaiah (who wrote the book of Isaiah) promises victory (2 Kings 19). Hezekiah, a man of faith, believes Isaiah's prophecy and God later extends his life (2 Kings 20). Nevertheless, Hezekiah's son, Manasseh, is deeply wicked and does everything his father had undone, following in Ahab's steps rather than David's. Manasseh even sacrifices his own son (probably to Molech or Chemosh) and sets up an idol in the Temple itself (2 Kings 21:1-9; but see 2 Chronicles 33). For his sin, God announces that Judah will face the same fate as Israel (2 Kings 21:13-14).

The last good king of Israel, Manasseh's grandson, is only eight years old when he takes the throne. Josiah raises money for the restoration of the Temple, and priests rediscover the Law after neglecting it for years (2 Kings 22:8; 11-13). For Josiah's faithfulness, God delays the destruction of Jerusalem until after his death (2 Kings 22:18-20). When Josiah dies in battle with Pharaoh Neco, the delays come to an end. Neco imprisons Josiah's son, Jehoahaz. The Pharoah forces Judah to pay tribute and sets up another of Josiah's sons as a puppet king. When Babylon replaces Egypt as the regional power, the king of Babylon, Nebuchadnezzar, takes captive the elites of Jerusalem (including Daniel and his companions) and installs his own puppet king, Zedekiah. Zedekiah rebels unsuccessfully against the king, and in 586 BC, the Babylonians destroy Jerusalem, its walls, and the Temple. The few Judeans who remain in the land soon flee (2 Kings 25:26). But there is hope! Jehoiachin lives out his days in relative comfort and fathers a son, Shealtiel, whose descendants carry on the line of David (Matthew 1:12; Luke 3:27).

Living It Out

Devotion: We might feel tempted to compare Elisha's call in 1 Kings 19:19-21 with Matthew 8:21-22 and Luke 9:59-60. Didn't Jesus forbid a man from burying his father before becoming a follower? Why did God allow Elisha to tell his parents goodbye? But such an interpretation misunderstands the passage in the Gospels. The man described in Matthew and Luke asks to delay the call indefinitely, for the rest of his father's life.[2] He wants to finish his own plans, get his affairs in order, and follow Jesus when it became more convenient. Consider Elisha, by contrast. He offers his livelihood to the Lord by burning his plow and sacrificing his oxen. When Jesus calls us, we must turn our backs on everything else and give him our complete devotion. The wicked kings failed to do this. Instead, they tried to serve both God and Baal. Remember Hezekiah and Josiah, who destroyed the land's idols and called for worship of God alone.

Wisdom: Solomon asked God for an understanding mind to govern the nation and to distinguish between good and evil. The word *wisdom* in the Bible refers to the skill of making the right decisions. Because Solomon asked for wisdom, God also rewarded him with all the things he didn't request.

Jesus said, "Seek the Kingdom of God above all else, and he will give you everything you need" (Luke 12:31). James 1:5

promises wisdom for those who ask. James 1:22 offers a warning that Solomon should have considered: "But don't just listen to God's word. You must do what it says. Otherwise, you are only fooling yourselves." Solomon had plenty of knowledge; he failed by refusing to act. Wisdom that does not begin with submission to God has no foundation and will not stand (Proverbs 9:10; Matthew 7:24-27).

Temple: See 1 and 2 Chronicles: Living It Out.

Questions for Review

1. How many righteous kings did the northern tribes have?

2. Describe how the people described in 1 and 2 Kings repeated some of the failures of Exodus, Numbers, and Judges. Why did they fall victim to the same temptations?

3. List the key factors that led to the division of the nation and its exile.

4. How does knowing the background of Samaria clarify passages such as John 4?

11

Jesus in the Former Prophets

It is no accident that Matthew's Gospel begins with a genealogy. God's purpose has continued to unfold in history since the beginning, and Jesus completes the story of Abraham, Moses, and David. The Bible does not disguise the warts of the heroes of the faith but portrays them as weaknesses that nevertheless could not overcome the faithfulness and grace of God.

When reading the Former Prophets, we can see the failures of these people as a reminder that we find our ultimate hope only in Jesus. The persistent rebellion under the judges and the divided monarchy should remind us that God remains faithful even when we falter (2 Timothy 2:12). God's high standards for worship also become obvious in these books. He is a holy God, and he rightly expects to be treated as such, but often is not. If Judges leaves us craving the righteous King David, the descendants of David and of Jeroboam cannot help but leave us craving King Jesus.

Several explicit comparisons may help: Jesus is the better Joshua (*Jesus* is a different form of the same name), who brings his people into the promises of God (2 Corinthians 1:20). David, as the faithful king after God's heart, gives us one of the clearest types of Christ. He defeated Goliath as the representative of his people. David crossed the Kidron when Ahithophel betrayed him (2 Samuel 15), and Jesus crossed the same brook when Judas betrayed him. David was anointed and destined to reign long before evil's authority came to an end (Hebrews 2:8-9). Jesus, the living Temple, is infinitely greater than Solomon or the magnificent building he constructed (Matthew 12:6, 42; John 2:19-22).

PART III

THE LATTER PROPHETS

WE OFTEN THINK of the Latter Prophets when we hear the word *prophecy*. Isaiah, Jeremiah, Ezekiel (the major writing prophets), and the so-called minor prophets all predicted the future, both short-term and long-term. But even here, they did not spend most of their time giving us an early edition of tomorrow's newspaper. As God's representatives, they called his people from sin to faithfulness. The sin of idolatry takes up most of their attention, illustrated through the metaphor of adultery. God had initiated a sacred love bond with his people, but they chased after other gods. Frequently, the prophets pointed out the absurdity of idolatry. It takes a hard heart to make a god with part of a log and then use the rest of the wood to cook breakfast.

The Latter Prophets describe the final decline of Israel and Judah, forecasting their exile and promising their eventual return.

Indeed, these prophets go beyond describing the nation's return to promise a better day when God will take away their sins and make a new covenant with them, at the same time reforming the whole creation. Unlike the Former Prophets, the Latter Prophets produce little narrative.

The three major prophets are **Isaiah**, **Jeremiah**, and **Ezekiel** (under the Jewish scheme, Daniel is placed among the Writings). Isaiah and Jeremiah prophesied primarily to Judah, whereas Ezekiel ministered largely to Israel. Their order is chronological. Isaiah prophesied in the eighth century BC, Jeremiah in the late seventh and early sixth, and Ezekiel in the early sixth.

The Minor Prophets are arranged in roughly chronological order: the pre-Assyrian prophets (**Hosea**, **Joel**, **Amos**, **Obadiah**, **Jonah**, **Micah**); the prophets during the decline of Assyria (**Nahum**, **Habakkuk**, **Zephaniah**); and the post-exilic prophets (**Haggai**, **Zechariah**, **Malachi**). In the Hebrew text, the minor prophets appear on one scroll, hence the name, "The Book of the Twelve."

12

Isaiah

[Isaiah's] whole pattern of thought has been affected by the tremendous contrast between the greatness of God and the corruption of humanity. But caught up with this contrast is the amazing paradox that if humanity will lay aside its pretensions to deity, the true God will raise us to fellowship with himself (Isaiah 57:15). These two thoughts form the heart of the book's theology.

JOHN N. OSWALT
The Book of Isaiah: Chapters 1–39

The Big Picture

Isaiah prophesied primarily from 740 to 690 BC, during the Israelite rebellion against Assyria (Isaiah 1:1). The New Testament quotes from Isaiah or alludes to it more than four hundred times.[1] The New Testament quotes more of Isaiah than any other book.[2] Isaiah moves between proclamations of judgment and promises of restoration, emphasizing that God will save a faithful remnant, not just from Israel but also from the Gentile nations. Sprinkled throughout are glimpses of a broader, cosmic redemption, culminating in new heavens and a new earth.

Digging Into Isaiah

Authorship

The book repeatedly identifies Isaiah, the son of Amoz, as its author (including Isaiah 1:1; 2:1; 7:3; 37:2; 39:3). Some commentators, including evangelicals, see a second author behind Isaiah 40–66 ("Deutero-Isaiah"), while others divide the book even further. This hypothesis depends on three lines of evidence: the different style of the book's end; the period covered (the book stretches over about two centuries); and the mention of Cyrus by name (born after the ministry of Isaiah). I believe one author is responsible for writing Isaiah. The mention of Cyrus by name should not surprise us if we serve the God who "can tell you the future before it even happens" (Isaiah 46:10). I see no reason why the author needed to be alive to write about events over a long period; and regardless of who wrote the book, the author did not live to see the new heavens and new earth (Isaiah 66:22-23). Stylistic differences may interest us, but we

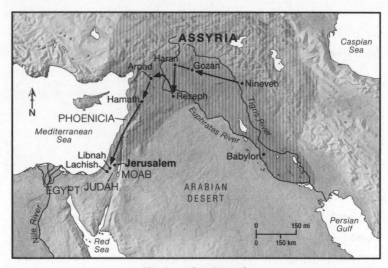

The Assyrian Assault

must give greater weight to the testimony of the New Testament, which attributes these latter chapters to Isaiah (Matthew 3:3; Mark 1:2; Luke 3:4-6; John 1:23; 12:38; Romans 10:16-21).[3]

Structure

1. Introduction (Isaiah 1–6)

2. Prophecies of Hope (Isaiah 7–12)

3. Judgments on the Nations (Isaiah 13–23)

4. Cosmic Judgment (Isaiah 24–27)

5. Woe on Judah and the Nations (Isaiah 28–35)

6. Hezekiah's Faith (Isaiah 36–39)

7. Hope in the Servant (Isaiah 40–48)

8. Servant Songs (Isaiah 49–55)

9. Invitation to True Worship (Isaiah 56–59)

10. Cosmic Redemption (Isaiah 60–66)

Introduction (Isaiah 1-6)

The book begins with a diatribe against Judah. Although God has blessed and cared for the people, they have rejected him.[4] Isaiah 5 vividly portrays the idea. The Lord compares himself to a landowner who carefully laid out a vineyard, gave it every advantage for growth, and yet found its grapes sour. "The nation of Israel is the vineyard of the LORD of Heaven's Armies. The people of Judah are his pleasant garden. He expected a crop of justice, but instead he found oppression. He expected to find righteousness, but instead he heard cries of violence" (Isaiah 5:7). This parable seems to inspire one Jesus gave (Matthew 21:33-46).

Isaiah's call begins with a theophany (a vision of God). He fears God's wrath as a sinner from a nation of sinners (Isaiah 6:5), but God purifies him and sends him out to preach, warning him that the people will not listen. Even this early section offers hope. God will preserve a faithful remnant (Isaiah 6:13).

Prophecies of Hope (Isaiah 7-12)

During the reign of King Ahaz, the king of Israel and the king of Syria make an alliance to attack the nation. Ahaz hears the rumor and Isaiah finds him at the aqueduct for the city, apparently already bracing himself for defense (Isaiah 7:3). But the Lord promises that the attack will never happen. In just sixty-five years, the northern tribes will no longer exist as a nation. God offers to let Ahaz choose a sign to verify his promise, but Ahaz refuses. So God himself chooses a sign: "The virgin will conceive a child! She will give birth to a son and will call him Immanuel" (Isaiah 7:14; Matthew 1:23).[5]

Quickly, we see that someone far more important than any ordinary child is coming. A child will come who will be called, "Wonderful Counselor, Mighty God, Everlasting Father, Prince of Peace" (Isaiah 9:6). A descendant of David called the Branch will rule righteously (Isaiah 11:1-5) and will usher in a period of supernatural peace, where the wolf and the lamb will live together (Isaiah 11:6), the nations will come to the Lord to be saved (Isaiah 11:10), and Israel will be reunited (Isaiah 11:13). You can see why some commentators call this book "The Gospel According to Isaiah." Jesus is hard to miss.

Judgments on the Nations (Isaiah 13-23)

Next come a series of judgments on the nations, beginning with Babylon (Isaiah 13:1–14:23), followed by judgments on many other enemies, including Assyria, Damascus, Israel, Ethiopia (Cush), Egypt, and Tyre. Scattered through these woes we see fascinating hints of a broader hope. The Lord will judge the nations, but a remnant of even the Egyptians will be a part of God's people (Isaiah 19:18-25). Some scholars have seen a reference to Satan as the power behind Babylon in Isaiah 14:12-17 (see also Ezekiel 28). The phrase translated "shining star" in Isaiah 14:12 is "Lucifer" in the early English translations and is the source of that traditional name for Satan.

Cosmic Judgment (Isaiah 24-27)

Isaiah 24 moves from these specific judgments to a much broader view of the earth's destruction. On that day, a banquet will replace the pain of this life, and death will be swallowed up forever (Isaiah 25:6-8). Resurrection, hinted at in earlier books, becomes vivid in 26:19: "But those who die in the LORD will live; their bodies will rise again! Those who sleep in the earth will rise up and sing for joy!" Leviathan (Isaiah 27:1; cf. Revelation 20:2) will be destroyed once and for all, and the vineyard from Isaiah 5 will become fruitful (Isaiah 27:1-6).

Woe on Judah and the Nations (Isaiah 28-35)

In the meantime, God's people will not escape divine judgment. Samaria and Jerusalem will be judged (Isaiah 28–29), and Judah's trust in the nations will lead to disaster (Isaiah 30:1-5). Real salvation can come only from the Lord (Isaiah 32:1; 33:22).

Hezekiah's Faith (Isaiah 36–39)
Isaiah 36–39 offers a historical side note in which Isaiah serves as God's representative to the righteous king, Hezekiah. King Sennacherib of Assyria (the nation that Ahaz had foolishly turned to) attacks Judah and sends a letter threatening to destroy Jerusalem. Hezekiah stretches out his letter before God (Isaiah 37:14), and God responds by destroying the Assyrian army (Isaiah 37:36). The Lord later heals Hezekiah's terminal illness. Hezekiah is an incredible model of faith, especially compared to Ahaz before him (Isaiah 38).

Hope in the Servant (Isaiah 40–48)
The poetry in the book's second half ascends to incredible heights. The character of the servant emerges (Isaiah 43:1-4; cf. Matthew 12:19-21), the one who will open the eyes of the blind and free the prisoners (Isaiah 42:6-7). Isaiah prophesies about Cyrus, a future king of Persia (Isaiah 45). The prophet refers to this Gentile as the Lord's anointed (the same word as Messiah/Christ). The God of Israel is King of all the nations, and even pagans who do not know him will serve his will. The Lord is the Savior of the world, and every knee will bend to him (Isaiah 45:22-23).

Servant Songs (Isaiah 49–55)
The servant songs revisit the servant of 43:1. At first, he seems to represent the whole nation (Isaiah 49:3), but this identification narrows to the faithful remnant of Israel (Isaiah 51:16). By Isaiah 52:13–53:12, this servant is clearly one person who will rescue the nation. The New Testament, of course, repeatedly identifies

this servant as Jesus (Matthew 8:17; Luke 22:37; Romans 4:25; 1 Peter 2:22-25).

Invitation to True Worship (Isaiah 56-59)

This section invites the nations to join united Israel to worship the true God (Isaiah 56:7-8) and turn from futile idolatry (Isaiah 57:13). Judah's failures of worship are more subtle than those of the nations, but their hypocritical displays do not impress the Lord (Isaiah 58:3-7). Still, God is ready and able to save if only they will repent (Isaiah 59:1-2, 20-21).

Cosmic Redemption (Isaiah 60-66)

The book concludes with beauty and glory. It predicts a day when Jerusalem will be restored, the nations will come to it, and God himself will be the light for the people (Isaiah 60:19; cf. Revelation 21:23). This glory culminates in a restored creation (Isaiah 65), where the wicked are finally judged and God restores the relationship between himself and his people, expressed in proper worship. The Lord will reverse the damage of the Fall, once and for all.

Living It Out

Anointed: The word *anointed* corresponds to *Messiah* in Hebrew and *Christ* in Greek. It refers to being set apart for an office through the smearing on of olive oil. We know it best for its reference to Jesus, who fulfills the three Old Testament offices of prophet, priest, and king (Isaiah 61:1; Luke 4:18). God calls Cyrus his anointed because the Persian king is not ultimately an independent agent, but an instrument of the sovereign God (Isaiah 45:1). We should never try to make politics our ultimate hope or allow it to bring us to despair. All world rulers ultimately remain subject to God's broader purpose (Daniel 2:21) under the authority of the true Anointed One (Romans 13:1).

Remnant: The book of Isaiah might feel depressing if it did not continually offer hope. Chapter after chapter warns of judgment on Gentile and Jew alike, but it also contains promises that God will never totally extinguish his people; in fact, he will add even Gentiles to their number. As the Lord told Elijah in 1 Kings 19, he has reserved for himself a people (Romans 11:1-6). In the New Testament, Jesus promises that the powers of hell will not overcome his church (Matthew 16:18). Things may get dark, persecution may come, but nothing can ever extinguish God's light in the world.

Questions for Review

1. Compare and contrast Cyrus and Jesus, both called the Lord's anointed.

2. Describe the major views on the authorship of the two main sections of Isaiah. Which do you find more plausible? Why?

3. How does Isaiah integrate the judgment of nations in his day with future cosmic judgment and restoration? How can we integrate those ideas?

4. Where do earlier books mention the idea of a faithful remnant? How does the rest of the Bible pick up on this theme?

13

Jeremiah

I should not have voluntarily chosen to be Jeremiah, the weeping prophet;
yet, methinks, no one of God's servants deserves greater honour than he
does, for he continued bravely to deliver his Master's message even when
none believed him, and all rejected his testimony.

CHARLES SPURGEON

The Big Picture

Jeremiah prophesied from 627 BC (the thirteenth year of the last righteous king, Josiah) until about 561 BC. Often called the weeping prophet, Jeremiah tragically saw no outward fruit over his long ministry. False prophets opposed Jeremiah, reassuring the people that the Lord would never allow his Temple to fall. Throughout his ministry, Jeremiah preached against the wickedness of the establishment. He declared that God would tear down the existing structures to plant the seeds of the future, when the Lord would send a new covenant to transform the people from the inside out. He prophesied about a century after the fall of the northern tribes, but often used the term "Israel" to refer to the whole nation.

Digging Into Jeremiah

1. Prologue (Jeremiah 1)

2. Prophecies against Judah and Jerusalem (Jeremiah 2–25)

3. Jeremiah vs. False Prophets (Jeremiah 26–29)

4. Prophecies of Comfort (Jeremiah 30–33)

5. Historical Interlude (Jeremiah 34–45)

6. Prophecies against Gentile Nations (Jeremiah 46–51)

7. Epilogue (Jeremiah 52)

Prologue (Jeremiah 1)
The book opens with Jeremiah's call as a prophet (Jeremiah 1:4-10). As Moses had worried about his speaking ability in Exodus 3, so the Lord had to reassure Jeremiah that his youth did not matter. He would speak God's words, and any strength he had to stand before the powerful would come from the Lord.

Prophecies against Judah and Jerusalem (Jeremiah 2-25)
This section begins with an attack on the idolatry characteristic of false prophets. Useless idols had pulled away the hearts of Judah, prompting them to abandon the "fountain of living water" and dig out "cracked cisterns that can hold no water at all" (Jeremiah 2:13). The people face the fate of all idolaters who worship worthless idols, "only to become worthless themselves" (Jeremiah 2:5).

The central metaphor for idolatry—spiritual adultery that abandons the covenant-love of the Lord—gets picked up in Jeremiah 2:20 and made especially clear in Jeremiah 3:1-5. Judah's sin is worse than Israel's because Judah saw Israel's judgment and still refuses to repent (Jeremiah 3:6-11). But their rejection will not be final. God promises that if they sincerely repent, they will not need to look back to the good old days. He will give them faithful leaders, Jerusalem itself will become the Lord's throne (without rebuilding the Ark), and Gentiles will gather to worship with reunited Israel (Jeremiah 3:14-18).

False prophets give false hope, claiming that the mere presence of the Temple will protect them (Jeremiah 7:1-13; 14:13; 23:32). Jeremiah weeps for the people until the Lord forbids him to pray for them anymore; God will not change his mind (Jeremiah 11:14; 14:11-12; 15:1). Meanwhile, the people Jeremiah loves plot to kill him for telling them the truth (Jeremiah 11:18-23; 15:15-21; 18:18-23; 20:1-2).

In Jeremiah 18, God sends Jeremiah to the potter's shop. As a potter changes his plans for the clay based on its imperfections, so the Lord will use Israel as a vessel of honor or shame based on its response to him. He plans disaster for them, so they need to repent and so prompt him to change course. But they do not; Israel is like a broken pot, headed for the trash heap (Jeremiah 19:10-13). Jeremiah scatters hope through all of this (Jeremiah 16:15; 23:1-8), but God inevitably pours out the cup of his wrath and the unrepentant nation begins seventy years of exile (Jeremiah 25).

Jeremiah vs. False Prophets (Jeremiah 26-29)
God temporarily thwarts the plots against Jeremiah, but another righteous prophet named Uriah is killed (Jeremiah 26:20-23). False prophets continue to tell the people what they want to

hear (Jeremiah 27:9-18; 29:26-28), including Hananiah (Jeremiah 28:1-4, 12-17) and Shemaiah (Jeremiah 29:24-32). Jeremiah continues to warn them that their sin *will* lead to judgment. The first wave of exiles to Babylon is only the beginning (Jeremiah 29:4-23).

The Babylonian Assault

Prophecies of Comfort (Jeremiah 30-33)

Despite all this, the Lord sends messages of hope to his people. Their exile will last a long time, but not forever (Jeremiah 30:10-11, 16-22). Matthew 2:18 picks up the metaphor of Rachel weeping for her children (Jeremiah 31:15-22). While Jeremiah uses the metaphor to refer to God comforting the nation's grief over those killed by the Assyrians and Babylonians, Matthew ties it to the slaughter of the infants in Bethlehem. The text does not specifically refer to the tragedy in Bethlehem, but it does fit with Jeremiah's themes coming to fruition in Jesus. The people may writhe in pain, but ultimate comfort is coming. God will send a new covenant to erase all the sins of the past and write his law on their hearts (Jeremiah 31:31-34; cf. Hebrews 8:8-12; 10:16-17; Romans 11:27).

Historical Interlude (Jeremiah 34-45)

This section is historical, covering events in the prophet's life from 605 BC to the fall of Jerusalem (Jeremiah 34–39), plus events after Jerusalem's fall (Jeremiah 40–45). Second Kings 24:16–25:30 and 2 Chronicles 36:10-18 describe the same events. Jeremiah points to models of faithlessness (slaves promised freedom and then denied it, Jeremiah 34:8-22) and faithfulness (the Recabites, Jeremiah 35), but when Jehoiakim replaces his father Josiah, the nation's leadership takes a final turn for the worse. Jeremiah has all his prophecies written down on a single scroll to give the people another chance to respond. Jehoiakim listens to them and then burns the scroll without remorse (Jeremiah 36:23-24). So Jeremiah dictates it all again, this time adding even more warnings of judgment.

When Jehoiachin dies, his son Zedekiah takes his place as the puppet king of Nebuchadnezzar. Judah turns to Pharaoh for help, but it provides only a temporary reprieve (Jeremiah 37:1-10). Jeremiah is arrested on false charges and imprisoned until Jerusalem falls (Jeremiah 37:11–38:6; 39:11– 40:6). Later, the prophet is taken to Egypt against his will by a group fleeing Nebuchadnezzar (Jeremiah 43:1-7). Jeremiah tells them that they will not be safe there and that the Lord will send Babylon even to Egypt to bring his judgment upon them (Jeremiah 43:8-13; 44:12).

Prophecies against Gentile Nations (Jeremiah 46-51)

With Judah defeated, Jeremiah prophesies about the wicked Gentile nations. Egypt (Jeremiah 46:2-28), Philistia (Jeremiah 47), Moab (Jeremiah 48), Ammon (Jeremiah 49:1-6), Edom (Jeremiah 49:7-22), Damascus (Jeremiah 49:23-27), Kedar and Hazor (Jeremiah 49:28-33), and Elam (Jeremiah 49:34-39) all will be judged. The climax of the book comes in the judgment of Babylon (Jeremiah 50–51) and the promise that Babylon's judgment will lead to the restoration of Israel (Jeremiah 50:19-20). The Lord uses these sinful nations to judge his people, but ultimately he will judge these instruments and restore his people.

Epilogue (Jeremiah 52)

Jeremiah 52 delivers a heart-wrenching, detailed epilogue describing the fall of Jerusalem and the destruction of the Temple. The author continues through the first half of the seventy-year exile (Jeremiah 52:31), showing the prophecies had already begun to occur. But once again, there is hope. Jehoiachin is given a special place and allowed to live out his days in relative comfort. The family line of David continues, barreling on toward the coming, perfect King.

Living It Out

Depravity: A wicked person's sin is as deeply embedded in his soul as skin color or a leopard's spots (Jeremiah 13:23). Our hearts are deceitful and unreliable guides for life (Jeremiah 17:9). No superficial solutions will do; only a new heart can solve the problem of sin (Jeremiah 32:38-41). This doctrine parallels in some ways Ephesians 2:3-8: We all have sinned and are children of wrath, but God graciously offers us new life in Christ. Even more powerful are the words of Jesus: "I tell you the truth, unless you are born again, you cannot see the Kingdom of God" (John 3:3). Modern philosophies blame our problems on outside factors (society, family, employer, etc.) and find the solution within (being true to ourselves, finding inner strength). The Bible presents the opposite case. Our problem lies within us, and we have only one solution: to recognize that we can never fix it on our own but need new hearts and new life in Christ.

New Covenant: Amid his warnings of judgment against the Israelites for continually breaking God's covenant, Jeremiah promised that a new covenant was coming (see Ezekiel 16; 36–37). This covenant would consist not of another set of laws to ignore, but would be written on transformed and forgiven hearts. Jesus inaugurated this covenant with his blood (Luke 22:20; 1 Corinthians 11:25) as the ultimate answer to depravity, because Jesus gives us a new set of desires and a new ability to carry them out (Jeremiah 32:40; Hebrews 9:15; 12:23). The false prophets expected to be protected because of God's Temple in Jerusalem, but we are protected because we are God's temple, indwelled by his Holy Spirit (John 16:7-14; Acts 1:6-8; 1 Corinthians 6:19).

Questions for Review

1. Does the description "weeping prophet" seem like a fair characterization of Jeremiah and his ministry? Why or why not?

2. What purpose does the historical interlude of Jeremiah 34-45 serve?

3. How does the new covenant idea build on what has come before? How does the New Testament further develop this theme?

14

Ezekiel

Though the mills of God grind slowly, yet they grind exceeding small;
Though with patience He stands waiting, with exactness grinds He all.

HENRY WADSWORTH LONGFELLOW
"Retribution"

The Big Picture

Ezekiel, a man from a priestly family, prophesied from about 593–
571 BC. Babylonian forces took him from Jerusalem to Babylon in
the second group of exiles. His prophecy shows a deep knowledge
of the Temple and the failures of the priests. It contains some of the
strongest condemnations of religious leaders of the period. Some
rabbis believed the book should be hidden from the unlearned,
lest apparent conflicts between Ezekiel and the Law confuse them.[1]
Because the prophet often used vivid imagery and sometimes acted
out his prophetic messages, Ezekiel is one of the more challenging books of the Old Testament to interpret. The New Testament
never explicitly quotes Ezekiel but does allude to it more than one
hundred times.[2]

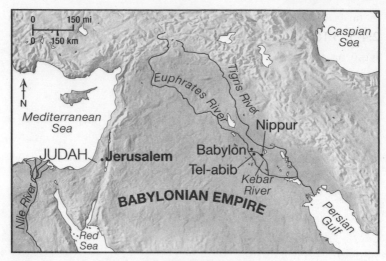

The Babylonian Exile

Digging Into Ezekiel

1. Judgment on Israel (Ezekiel 1–24)
    a. The Beginning of Ezekiel's Ministry (Ezekiel 1–5)
    b. The Day of the LORD (Ezekiel 6–7)
    c. The Departure of God's Glory (Ezekiel 8–11)
    d. Judgment on Jerusalem (Ezekiel 12–24)

2. Judgment on the Nations (Ezekiel 25–32)

3. Restoration of Israel (Ezekiel 33–48)

Judgment on Israel (Ezekiel 1-24)

Ezekiel's visions begin with a theophany (a vision of God) and a commissioning. God does not promise him success but calls him to faithfully warn the people, whether they obey or not (Ezekiel 2:4-5; 3:16-19). The Lord gives Ezekiel visual prophecies, from lying on his side for more than a year (Ezekiel 4:4-6) to using his shorn hair to symbolize the destruction, exile, and preserved remnant of Israel (Ezekiel 5:1-13).

In chapters 8–11, Ezekiel describes the glory of God leaving the Temple. God's presence had been with the nation from the time the people left Egypt, settling on the Tabernacle and then the Temple. Now, God describes them as "[driving] me from my Temple" (Ezekiel 8:6), and his glory leaves. Later Jewish rabbis called this visible glory the *shekinah*, although the word does not appear in the Bible. The Lord's glory departs the Temple and goes to the Mount of Olives (Ezekiel 11:22-23). Someday it will return (Zechariah 14:4).

Ezekiel then somberly packs his bags, preparing to go into exile, and moves outside the city (Ezekiel 12:3). This visual picture of the nation's future does not shake the people, who continue to listen to false prophets (Ezekiel 13). The false prophets undoubtedly use several arguments to reassure the people, including the idea that their trouble was not their fault. They quoted a proverb: "The parents have eaten sour grapes, but their children's mouths pucker at the taste" (Ezekiel 18:2). God rebukes them for this nonsense. They will suffer for *their* sin, not the sin of their parents. God does not desire anyone's death, but the one who sins will die (Ezekiel 18:23-32).

When Ezekiel's wife dies (Ezekiel 24:15-27), the Lord tells him not to weep, to mourn, or to accept any comfort. His deep pain pictures Israel's future grief for its sins. The things they consider unshakable will be taken from them and their hearts will groan over their sin.

Judgment on the Nations (Ezekiel 25-32)

Ezekiel 25 begins a series of judgments on the nations: Ammon; Moab and Edom; Philistia; Tyre; Sidon; and Egypt. God will destroy each of these nations for their sin. Some Bible students have noted that the description of the King of Tyre in Ezekiel 28 seems to go beyond what could be said of an ordinary person; they see it as a reference to Satan, the demonic power behind Tyre (see also Isaiah 14). Though the New Testament never makes this connection explicit, many church fathers endorsed it.[3]

God has one primary goal in judging the nations—to teach Israel not to trust anyone but him (Ezekiel 29:13-16). If the Lord can so easily crush the nations to whom Israel had turned, then why not go to the Lord directly for deliverance? These warnings, like the others, go unheeded.

Restoration of Israel (Ezekiel 33-48)

When the prophet returns his focus to the nation, his voice grows somber. Jerusalem has fallen (Ezekiel 33:21). Some people continue to live in the land, thinking that they can hide out there and enjoy the land in their own power. For their presumption, God strikes them down (Ezekiel 33:21-29). The people listen to Ezekiel for entertainment but do not obey (much as Herod would later listen to John the Baptist, Mark 6:20). God cannot restore them until they stop their hypocrisy.

Still, God will search for them like a shepherd rescuing his sheep (Ezekiel 34). The Lord will not merely save them from the consequences of sin, but create a new covenant with them, written on their hearts by his Spirit (Ezekiel 36:25-27). He promises to restore them, not because of their works, but because of his grace (Ezekiel 36:32). Like old, dried-out bones brought back to life, Israel will live again (Ezekiel 37).

The controversial chapters of Ezekiel 40–48 describe a new Temple in extraordinary detail, as evidence that God will return to his people. Evangelicals have debated three main theories explaining this Temple. One treats it as a literal temple, built during the reign of Christ as described in Revelation 20:1-7. Another views the Temple as a metaphor for the church (1 Peter 2:5). The last sees the prophecy as conditional: Had the nation remained faithful, its people would have built this Temple, but their unbelief stopped it. No easy solution exists, since Ezekiel describes Levites making animal sacrifices to atone for sin (Ezekiel 44:15; 45:17), which seems to contradict Hebrews 7:12-28.

Nothing in the text, however, sees the promise as conditional. And what metaphorical significance could such detailed regulations have? Regardless, the central theme remains clear. God's presence left Israel because of its wickedness, but a new prince is coming and God's presence will return. Reconciliation may seem slow, but it will happen.

Living It Out

Painful Truth: Ezekiel's biggest opponents, the false prophets, told the people what they wanted to hear instead of the truth. They promised that God would not remove his people from the land and would never allow anyone to destroy his Temple. This false sense of security allowed the people to continue in their sins, even as judgment drew ever closer. Paul warns against a time when people will look for teachers eager to tell them "whatever their itching ears want to hear" (2 Timothy 4:3). The same problem existed long before Ezekiel's day. Generations before, Rehoboam had shopped around for someone to endorse his own sinful desires (1 Kings 12:8). Sometimes those who genuinely love us must tell us things we would rather not hear. The wise will receive correction and learn from it, while the foolish will turn away to kinder words from crueler hearts (Proverbs 27:6).

Watchman: God describes Ezekiel as a watchman on the city's wall, responsible to warn the people of danger. If he fails, their blood is on his hands. If he does warn them and they ignore him, they are responsible for their own fate (Ezekiel 33:1-9). The New Testament gives us a similar charge. God tells us to share the gospel, but we are not ultimately responsible for the results (see Luke 10:16; cf. Paul's example in Acts 20:26-27). That encourages me! Our part is to be faithful; God gives the increase (1 Corinthians 3:7).

Worship: The new Temple presents us with one of the most challenging passages to interpret in Ezekiel. Will animal sacrifices happen again in the future? Is this some kind of detailed metaphor? Regardless of where you fall on these questions, Ezekiel makes the restoration of proper worship one of his major themes. The people need a new priest, a restored sanctuary, and the return of God's presence. In Jesus, the great High Priest (Hebrews 5:5), we have access to God in spirit and truth (John 4). God's presence even dwells in us, both individually (1 Corinthians 6:19) and corporately (1 Corinthians 3:16), enabling us to worship at all times. God designed us to worship, and we will either worship the true God or become "a perpetual forge of idols."[4]

Questions for Review

1. Why is the loss of God's presence and its future restoration so central to Ezekiel's theology?

2. Describe Ezekiel's role as a "watchman." How does this apply to modern Christians?

3. How did Ezekiel employ visible actions to bring to life and reinforce his prophecies?

15

The Minor Prophets

*I have trouble with the Minor Prophets sometimes, finding them,
but I assure you they are called Minor Prophets only because of the length
of their message, not because of the importance of their message.*

ADRIAN ROGERS

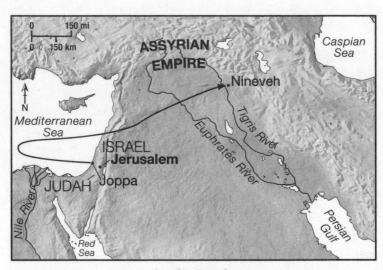

Jonah's Travels

The Big Picture

The Minor Prophets, called the "Book of the Twelve" in the Jewish tradition, have a remarkable flow between them. The first six prophets (Hosea—Micah) emphasize the sin of Israel and the nations, the following three (Nahum—Zephaniah) focus on God's judgment on the Day of the Lord, and the final three (Haggai—Malachi) describe the future restoration.[1] Though they do not appear in strict chronological order, Hosea—Micah are traditionally dated as pre-Assyrian exile, Nahum—Zephaniah were written during the decline of Assyria, and Haggai—Malachi belong to a period after the return from Babylon.

Digging Into the Minor Prophets

Hosea

By about 756–722 BC, during the days of Hosea's prophetic activity, the nation of Israel had grown prosperous and placed its faith in Assyria instead of God (Hosea 8:8-9; 12:1). The nation's prosperity convinced the people they did not need to return to the Lord. Only Hosea among the writing prophets was both from Israel and prophesied to Israel. In the first three chapters, Hosea's wife (Gomer) commits adultery, a vivid metaphor for Israel's worship of other gods. Yet Gomer is restored, foreshadowing the ultimate reconciliation of the nation to the Lord. Chapters 4–14 feature sermons about the nation in three sections: chapters 4–7 condemn Israel's apostasy; chapters 8–10 describe the punishment; and chapters 11–14 promise the future restoration.

Joel

Some scholars believe Joel wrote during the reign of Joash (820 BC), whereas others contend his book was written after the return from exile (580 BC).² A locust plague has just swept the land, and Joel emphasizes that it is nothing compared to the coming Day of the Lord (Joel 1:2-3, 15). An unstoppable force, led by the Lord himself, will raze the land (Joel 2:1-11). But there is hope! Joel calls the people to genuine repentance: "Don't tear your clothing in your grief, but tear your hearts instead. Return to the LORD your God, for he is merciful and compassionate" (Joel 2:13; cf. Deuteronomy 30:1-6). If they repent, God will restore what the locusts destroyed and will personally return (Joel 2:25-27).

In Acts 2:16-21, Peter quotes the promise of Joel 2:29-32, declaring that the Holy Spirit's descent on Pentecost fulfilled Joel's prophecy. The prophecy was not entirely fulfilled, however, because many other events Joel described have not yet occurred. This phenomenon is called "prophetic foreshortening," where events far distant from one another are described as if close together. Like many Old Testament prophets, Joel does not distinguish between events at the first and second coming of Christ.

The book concludes with a glimmer of hope. God will judge Israel, but he will also judge the nations that oppressed them. When the Lord restores his people, he will judge and destroy their enemies (Joel 3).

Amos

The earthquake of Amos 1:1 allows us to firmly date the book to 760–750 BC. Like Hosea, Amos prophesies during a time of material prosperity but spiritual poverty. Amos is from Judah but prophesies in Israel. His prophecy targets two main sins: idolatry and social injustice. Although the New Testament cites Amos only twice (Acts 7:42-43; cf. Amos 5:25-27; Acts 15:16-17; cf. Amos 9:11-12), Amos clearly emphasizes the relationship between proper worship and proper treatment of our neighbors (Matthew 22:36-40; 1 John 3:17).

Amos begins with a series of prophecies against Israel's enemies, including Judah (1:1–2:5). If his audience enjoys his condemnation of their enemies, they probably do not appreciate it when he turns his eyes to Israel (Amos 2:6-16). Although the Israelites have God's Word and the prophets, they behave worse than their enemies, the Philistines and the Egyptians (Amos 3). He compares the lavish lifestyles of the women of Samaria to fattened cows (Amos 4:1-3) and facetiously mocks them for their expertise in ritual but ignorance of holiness (Amos 4:4-13). He sings a funeral dirge over them, for although they seem alive and prosperous, they will never enjoy it until they turn from their idolatry and their oppression. All their worship and wealth are nothing but hypocrisy that God will one day reveal (Amos 5).

Amos 7:1–9:10 describes five visions of judgment. After each of the first two (locusts and fire), Amos prays for mercy and God relents. The third vision (a plumb line) shows that God will judge the people by his absolute standards and that justice will no longer delay. A vision of ripe fruit, ready for harvest, shows the imminence of judgment, introduced by another list of the nation's sins. The final vision shows God beside the altar, bringing the Temple down on the people. Even in his judgment, however, the Lord promises to preserve a remnant (Amos 9:8). The book concludes with a promise of lasting restoration (Amos 9:11-15).

Obadiah

Obadiah, the shortest book in the Bible, was written in 587 BC as a straightforward oracle of judgment against Edom for its hatred of Israel. The Edomites, descendants of Esau, Jacob's brother, never showed any compassion to Israel. Their destruction prefigured the judgment of Gentile nations at the time of Israel's restoration. The pagans might arrogantly believe they lie beyond God's reach, but "the LORD himself will be king" (Obadiah 1:21).

Jonah

Written around 750 BC, probably by Jonah himself, this book optimistically shows God's grace and realistically shows the weaknesses of his servants. The Lord sends Jonah to Nineveh, a major city in Assyria that later would become the empire's capital. It reads more like the Former Prophets than the Latter Prophets, teaching spiritual principles through sacred history rather than recording the prophet's words. Although some have found a fish swallowing a man unbelievable, Jesus referred to it as history (Luke 11:29), and 2 Kings 14:25 lists Jonah as an actual prophet.

The drama takes place in four acts. First, God calls Jonah to preach to Nineveh (Jonah 1). He chooses instead to go to Tarshish, one thousand miles in the wrong direction (see the map at the beginning of the chapter). God sends a storm to his ship, and the sailors throw him overboard, where a specially prepared fish swallows him.

Second, after three days and three nights, Jonah prays from the belly of the fish, his prayer recorded as a psalm and stylized as if spoken from the heart of Sheol (the grave, Jonah 2). Jonah's figurative death and resurrection picture the real death and resurrection of Jesus (Matthew 12:39).

Third, God gives Jonah a second chance to obey (Jonah 3). He does and, amazingly, the Ninevites repent. We do not know if they come to saving faith, but at least they turn from their wickedness and God stops his judgment.

Finally, Jonah grows angry at God for showing mercy to the

hated Ninevites (Jonah 4). He only reluctantly preaches to these notoriously cruel people because he fears that God will forgive them. God prepares a plant to shade Jonah and then kills it. When the prophet gets upset, the Lord asks Jonah whether a plant deserves more pity than a city full of human beings. The God of all the earth eagerly forgives all who turn from their sin. Will his people show the same compassion?

Micah

Micah prophesies between 740 and 686 BC (from Hezekiah to Jotham) and addresses both Israel and Judah. A contemporary of Isaiah, his prophecies alternate between judgment and hope. Christians know Micah best as the book that predicts the birth of Jesus in Bethlehem (Micah 5:2; cf. Matthew 2:4-6; Luke 2:1-7). Micah also has the unique distinction of being the only prophet quoted by name in another prophet's writing (Micah 3:12; cf. Jeremiah 26:18-19). Micah prophesies against both Judah and Israel (specifically against Jerusalem and Samaria, the respective capitals of the two nations).

By the time of Micah's ministry, the wealth of Hosea and Amos a generation earlier had faded; only the sin remained. Social injustice and idolatry at the highest levels of society still put the people on a path to disaster. His prophecy breaks into three cycles (chapters 1–2; chapters 3–5; and chapters 6–7), each opening with warnings of judgment and concluding with a hope of salvation. The first two salvation oracles center on a coming king unlike the wicked rulers of Micah's day. That King will graciously shepherd his people (Micah 2:12-13; 5:4-5). In the final salvation oracle, the Lord is the one who will shepherd and lead his people (Micah 7:14). Of course, we know the promised shepherd is both God and man—the son of David and the Son of God, Jesus Christ.

Nahum

Probably writing shortly before 612 BC (when Nineveh falls), but definitely after 663 BC (when the fall of Thebes takes place, described in Nahum 3:8-10), Nahum announces the fall of Nineveh, by then the capital of Assyria. Assyria has already conquered Israel (722 BC) and Nineveh's repentance under Jonah's preaching a century earlier is long forgotten.

The book has a simple structure. The first chapter praises the holiness and might of the Lord, who will judge his enemies. The second chapter predicts the judgment of Nineveh in vivid terms and describes the city as razed by the Lord. Although Assyria was God's instrument to judge Israel, it, too, will be judged for its sin. As with Joseph in Genesis, God works all things together for good (Romans 8:28). Nahum 3 reflects on the fall of the city, showing its shame and guilt. As Jonah shows, though God is patient and merciful, he is also holy and righteous. People today would do well to consider that God's patience does not mean that he will delay his judgment forever (Hebrews 10:37; 2 Peter 3:9).

Habakkuk

The prophet Habakkuk prophesies shortly before 600 BC (the invasion predicted in Habakkuk 1:6 happened in about 598 BC). This book logically follows after Nahum, which showed that God's patience with Nineveh had ended. Habakkuk is concerned about how much longer the Lord will tolerate Judah's sin. He opens his book by complaining to God: *How long?* (Habakkuk 1:1-4). God responds that it will not be long; the Babylonians will come and punish Israel (Habakkuk 1:5-11). Habakkuk questions God again, this time asking for reassurance that the Babylonians will come to purify the people, not to destroy them (Habakkuk 1:12–2:1). In his second reply, God promises him that the tables will turn and

Babylon's former captives will mock them when Babylon itself is judged (Habakkuk 2:2-20). Habakkuk 3 records a song of hope for ultimate salvation. Times may grow rough, but God will ultimately restore his people.

Habakkuk's most famous verse is undoubtedly 2:4, which is quoted in Romans 1:17, Galatians 3:11, and Hebrews 10:38. A quick comparison of those passages shows that the New Testament speaks of *faith*, while God in Habakkuk speaks of *faithfulness*. How can Paul and the author of Hebrews use this text to support the idea of salvation apart from works? Moisés Silva argues persuasively that such an assertion betrays a false dichotomy: "Faith involves waiting for fulfillment and thus is always in danger of being shaken; therefore, steadiness and constancy are of its essence . . . for Habakkuk, there was no such dichotomy between faith and faithfulness as we often assume."[3] The New Testament accurately picks up his point: The wicked trust in themselves and live accordingly, while the righteous trust God and live accordingly. With all the prophets, Habakkuk affirms that God's people must not separate proper worship and proper living.

Zephaniah

Zephaniah, writing in roughly 630–620 BC, prophesies in Judah after Isaiah but before Jeremiah (perhaps overlapping with the beginning of Jeremiah's ministry). He prophesies during the reign of the last righteous king, Josiah, but his comments about idolatry indicate that his ministry at least began before Josiah's reforms (remember that Josiah was only eight when he became king, see 2 Kings 22:1; 2 Chronicles 34:1). Zephaniah directs the first section of his prophecy (Zephaniah 1:1–2:3) at Judah. The Day of the Lord is coming quickly, and the people will be judged for their wickedness (Zephaniah 1:14). But he offers a glimmer of hope. If the people repent before the Day of Judgment, they can be protected (Zephaniah 2:1-3).

The second section turns to Israel's enemies (Zephaniah 2:4-15) before the third section returns to Jerusalem (Zephaniah 3). The Lord has been faithful to them, but they are rebellious and wicked. They have seen all of his judgments on the pagans and yet still fail to repent (Zephaniah 3:7). Finally, God offers a broader hope. All nations will worship together (Zephaniah 3:9) alongside the faithful remnant of Israel (Zephaniah 3:10-13). The Lord himself will come to dwell among them and restore their hearts (Zephaniah 3:16-17).

Haggai

Three dates allow us to most naturally outline Haggai into four sections: August 29, the call to rebuild the Temple (Haggai 1); October 17, the promise of a better temple (Haggai 2:1-9); December 18, the restoration of God's blessing (Haggai 2:10-17); and later on December 18, the promise to Zerubbabel (Haggai 2:18-23).

The people returned to the land in 538 BC but have not yet rebuilt the Temple. By prioritizing the construction of their own homes, they have voided God's blessing on anything they do (Haggai 1:5-6, 9-11). If they rebuild the Temple, God will take care of their other needs (a principle repeated in Matthew 6:33). The governor and the high priest receive the message first, a pleasant change from the wicked shepherds of the pre-exilic prophets. Once reconstruction begins, people grieve at the inferiority of the rebuilt Temple (Haggai 2:3), but the Lord reassures them that his Spirit is with them, which is enough (Haggai 2:5). The time will come when he will make the Temple greater than it has ever been, shaking the nations and bringing their glory to his house

(Haggai 2:6-9; cf. Hebrews 12:26-27). Haggai 2:10-19 seems to reflect on the time before the rebuilding of the Temple when their sin contaminated everything they did. It promises that when they lay the foundation of the Temple, his presence will bless them. On that same day, God promises the governor of Judah, Zerubbabel, that he will become God's signet ring—a sign of greater things to come (Haggai 2:23).

Zechariah

The writer of the longest book of the minor prophets, Zechariah was a contemporary of Haggai (Ezra 5:1; 6:14). He begins writing in October–November of 520 BC, but we do not know how long his ministry lasts. The book is familiar to Christians for its prophecies of the triumphal entry (Zechariah 9:9; cf. Matthew 21:5; John 12:15), the scattering of the apostles (Zechariah 13:7; cf. Mark 14:27), and the future when the Israelites will "look on me whom they have pierced" (Zechariah 12:10; cf. John 19:37). But Revelation alludes to the book of Zechariah at least nineteen times,[4] and the rest of the New Testament echoes it many times.[5] This extremely important book too often gets neglected because of its placement toward the end of the minor prophets.

Two major sections define the book: chapters 1–8 and 9–14.[6] After an introduction (Zechariah 1:1-6), Zechariah reports eight visions and their explanations (Zechariah 1:7–6:8). These visions describe the imminence of God's judgment on the nations (Zechariah 1:7-17), the broken power of the nations that had exiled Israel and Judah (Zechariah 1:18-21), the return of the exiles (Zechariah 2), the preparation of the high priest Joshua[7] over Satan's accusations (Zechariah 3), the two anointed ones (Zechariah 4), the curse of the wicked in the land (Zechariah 5:1-4), the removal of the nation's past sins (Zechariah 5:5-11), the four chariots patrolling the earth (Zechariah 6:1-8), and the crowning of the high priest Joshua (Zechariah 6:9-15). Zechariah 7–8 emphasizes the importance of authentic worship, in contrast to the hypocritical ritualism of the people's ancestors.

Though each of these divisions is fairly easy to understand, Zechariah 6:12-13 often trips up Christian readers. Is the priest, Joshua, the Branch, as promised in Jeremiah 23? Did Joshua rule as both priest and king? Grammatically, "Branch" cannot apply to Joshua; the work described most closely matches Zerubbabel.[8] But Zerubbabel is no perfect match either. Both Zerubbabel and Joshua function as partial symbols of the coming Jesus.

The second major division of Zechariah describes the coming of a future king who will ride into Jerusalem on a donkey and free the prisoners (Zechariah 9:9-17). God promises to judge the wicked rulers who left his people without a shepherd (Zechariah 10:1-3; cf. Numbers 27:17; 1 Kings 22:17; Matthew 9:36) and to bless the remnant (Zechariah 10:4-12). Chapter 11 provides a somber interlude: The people reject him (Zechariah 11:8) and value him at thirty pieces of silver (Zechariah 11:12-13; cf. Matthew 27:6-10). They will be given over to a wicked ruler who will abuse them (Zechariah 11:14-17), but things will change. They will receive a spirit of grace and look on the Lord whom they have pierced (Zechariah 12:10-11) and be restored (Luke 13:35; Romans 11:26). This verse, applied to Jesus in John 19:37 and Revelation 1:7, gives us one of the most powerful proofs of the doctrine of the Trinity in the Bible. Jesus and the Lord are one! Chapter 13 promises a day when no wickedness will be tolerated in the land, while chapter 14 tells of the day when the Lord will stand on the Mount of Olives (where his presence had departed in Ezekiel) with all his holy ones

(Zechariah 14:1-5). The wicked will be judged, the survivors of the nations will come to worship the Lord, and even the most mundane things will be set apart as holy (Zechariah 14:16-21). A better day is coming!

Malachi

Malachi, the final Old Testament prophet, dates to about 430 BC. After his ministry, four centuries of prophetic silence ensue until the arrival of John the Baptist. By the time Malachi writes, the people had returned from exile more than a hundred years before. How much longer would they have to wait on the promises God had given? Malachi answers with a series of dialogues between God and the people, explaining that they are not yet ready. They bring sacrifices unworthy of the Lord's honor (Malachi 1:6-14); the priests have abandoned their responsibilities (Malachi 2:1-9); and the men have divorced their wives to marry idolatrous women (Malachi 2:10-17). God answers by sending a messenger to prepare the way before his sudden return to his Temple (Malachi 3:1; although God's presence was among them, according to Haggai 1:13, the Lord never returned with the same visible glory as before). Malachi calls the people to repent of their social sins (Malachi 3:5), their religious sins (Malachi 3:6-12), and their personal sins (Malachi 3:13-18). Like most of the prophets, Malachi describes the coming Day of the Lord in two ways. For the wicked, it will be a consuming fire. For the righteous, it will be a warm, healing sun. He calls on the people to obey the Law and keep an eye out for the prophet Elijah, who will return to call the people to repentance.

In the standard English order, Malachi is the last book of the Old Testament, and it ends on a cliff-hanger (Malachi 4:5-6). When the prophet Elijah comes to prepare the way of the Lord, how will the people respond? What will it be like when the Lord finally comes to make all things right? We already noticed that Genesis and the Pentateuch each end with lingering questions; and 2 Chronicles (the final book of the Hebrew Bible) follows the same pattern (2 Chronicles 35:22-23). The Old Testament builds up our longing for the coming of Jesus in the Gospels, just as the endings of the Gospels, Acts, and Revelation leave us eager for his return.

Living It Out

The Day of the Lord: The prophets warn of a coming Day of Judgment, when God's wrath will be fully revealed. Ordinary judgments could give foretastes of it (Lamentations 2:22), but the final judgment of the world will look like nothing before it (Joel 3:14-21; Malachi 4:5). Whether the Day of the Lord will be a positive or a negative experience depends entirely on the individual. The faithful will see their enemies judged and their hearts cleansed, and they will enter into the rest of their Savior. The wicked will face judgment and destruction. No one will escape the Day of the Lord on the basis of their national identity alone (Amos 5:18-20); each person must stand before God personally.

The New Testament speaks about the day of Christ (1 Corinthians 1:8; Philippians 2:16), reinforcing the idea of Jesus as the ultimate judge (John 5:22). We all will be judged; none will be able to claim innocence (Romans 3:23). Our only possible salvation is to plead the blood of Jesus (Romans 5:9). For believers, the return of Christ brings no cause for fear, as it is our greatest hope (2 Timothy 4:8; Titus 2:13; 1 John 3:1-3).

Spiritual Adultery: Idolatry is frequently pictured as spiritual adultery—that's one of the Bible's most visceral metaphors for the sin of forsaking God for something else. Hosea may be the best-known example here (or Ezekiel 16 in the major prophets), but we see the theme often repeated. God is no more willing to share our love than a husband or wife would be. He deserves an exclusive and devoted kind of love, which means that letting our hearts follow other gods deeply grieves him. James 4:4-5 repeats the same idea in the New Testament: "You adulterers! Don't you realize that friendship with the world makes you an enemy of God? I say it again: If you want to be a friend of the world, you make yourself an enemy of God. Do you think the Scriptures have no meaning? They say that God is passionate that the spirit he has placed within us should be faithful to him."

The New Testament uses the metaphor of a pure bride, ready to wed Christ, to picture the church (2 Corinthians 11:2-3; Ephesians 5:22-33; Revelation 19:7; 21:1-9; 22:17). We should not think of sin as a minor blip in our lives, but as unfaithfulness to the one who has remained completely loving and faithful to us. Sin is no mere legal violation, but a deep betrayal.

Hope for the World: Amazingly, the minor prophets regularly promise hope for Gentiles. While the pagan nations that opposed Israel will be judged, a remnant of the nations will come to worship the Lord, just as Israel also had a faithful remnant. The Bible had described this theme earlier (Isaiah 49:6), but it really stands out in these short books. We should feel reassured that the great commission is no afterthought. God has always intended to offer the gospel to the nations, and we have the honor of being a part of that (Titus 1:3). When we read or teach from the Minor Prophets, the warnings of coming judgment should motivate us to take the Good News to those who have not yet heard (Romans 13:11-14; 2 Corinthians 6:2).

Questions for Review

1. Which prophets addressed foreign nations? Which addressed Israel? Which addressed Judah?

2. How did the prophets integrate promises of judgment and restoration? Is salvation possible without judgment?

3. In what sense are Jonah and Haggai prophecy?

16

Jesus in the Latter Prophets

WE FIND JESUS in the Old Testament more easily in the Latter Prophets than probably anywhere else. So many of their prophecies directly reference his work. Students must carefully discern which verses refer to the first coming of Christ and which refer to the second, because the prophets often move seamlessly between both. Skeptics might find this a little too convenient and claim that we are trying to explain away prophecies that Jesus should have fulfilled in the first century, but carefully reading the Latter Prophets undermines this false idea. The prophets not only combined the first and second comings of Christ, they sometimes wove prophecies between the immediate future and the ultimate future. If they had somehow expected the world to end with the fall of Jerusalem or Babylon, it strains credulity to imagine that the Jewish people would have left these books in the canon, since in that case the predictions would have failed just a few years later. Instead, we see that the prophets often combine future events *thematically*, not always chronologically. Short-term judgments, Christ's earthly ministry, and his return all demonstrate the same fundamental truths about God's character.

When looking for Jesus in the Latter Prophets, we must look first for the immediate fulfillment of God's promises. Though the ultimate culmination might go beyond the author's day, it always moves in the same direction. Reading through the prophets and picking up their train of thought and their emphases will keep us from pulling their words out of context and forcing them to fit with our own ideas. But if our concerns line up with their concerns, we can be confident we are on the right track.

Second, we must remember that the prophets are not primarily foretellers of the future, but rather *forthtellers*, announcing God's word and will. God wants to conform us to the character of Jesus, not merely tell us about him. Thus, we should look for the character of Jesus as revealed in the prophets, in both love and holiness, and see how this should shape the way we live.

Finally, we should realize that the entire Bible centers on Christ (Luke 24:32; John 5:39). Understood correctly, countless passages point directly to Christ—and God's faithfulness to his promises about the first coming should reassure us about the Second Coming and every other part of God's Word.

PART IV

THE WRITINGS

THE WRITINGS MAKE UP the final section in the Jewish canon. This incredibly diverse portion of Scripture contains poetry composed over millennia (Psalms, Lamentations, and Song of Songs), wisdom literature in various forms (Proverbs, Ecclesiastes, and Job), histories (Ruth, Esther, Ezra, and Nehemiah), a unique kind of literature called apocalyptic (Daniel), and a recitation of the same events described in 1 Samuel—2 Kings (1–2 Chronicles), which leaves many readers wondering why we need both. In many ways, this final section applies what has come before in the Bible. How did the people live out the principles given in the Law and the Prophets?

If these books seem messy and disconnected, maybe that's because our lives look the same way. No one can deny, however, that many of these books are among the most loved in the Bible.

We mourn with David, love with Solomon, question with Job, and reflect on the past with the Chronicler. I have my great-grandfather's pocket Bible from his time in the Second World War that contains the New Testament and Psalms. These books speak to our hearts, and the better we study and understand them, the more fully we can appreciate this part of God's Word.

Hebrew poetry (such as Psalms, Proverbs, and Job) depends on parallel *ideas* rather than similar sounds. In a couplet, the simplest form of parallel structure, the two lines either repeat the same idea (a synonymous couplet), develop an idea (a synthetic couplet), or contrast with each other (an antithetical couplet).

Psalm 15:1 provides an example of a synonymous couplet: "Who may worship in your sanctuary, LORD? / Who may enter your presence on your holy hill?"

Psalm 37:25 shows us a synthetic couplet (where the second line builds on the first): "Yet I have never seen the godly abandoned / or their children begging for bread."

Psalm 145:20 features an antithetical couplet: "The LORD protects all those who love him / but he destroys the wicked."

More complex examples use couplets assembled in larger structures (look for the relationships between the lines in Psalm 3:1-4). Remain alert for these relationships, just as you look for the flow of a narrative in the Former Prophets or the flow of an argument in the New Testament epistles.

Another key element of Hebrew poetry, the chiasm (or chiasmus), features a first line that corresponds to the last, a second that corresponds to the second to last, etc. This structure emphasizes the middle element, which may or may not be a pair. Proverbs 18:6-7 (NIV) provides a good example, where "lips" in the first and last lines correspond, and "mouths" connects the inner two lines. It emphasizes the fate of fools: beating and ruin.

A *The lips of fools bring them strife,*

B *and their mouths invite a beating.*

B´ *The mouths of fools are their undoing,*

A´ *and their lips are a snare to their very lives.*

17

Psalms

I sing for I cannot be silent;
His love is the theme of my song.
FANNY CROSBY
"Redeemed, How I Love to Proclaim It!"

The Big Picture

It took over a millennium to write the Psalms, the hymnbook of ancient Israel. Our word *psalm* comes from the Greek word for *song*, but the Hebrew title for the book is "Praises." Israel used this collection of songs to praise the Lord throughout its history. Moses wrote the earliest psalm (Psalm 90) in the fifteenth century BC, while an unknown writer composed the latest, Psalm 126, after the nation's return from exile in the fifth century BC. That means these poems were written over approximately the same time span as the rest of the Old Testament.

More psalms are attributed to David than to any other author (seventy-three, with twelve more attributed to him in the LXX), while twelve are attributed to Asaph (David's chief musician, 1 Chronicles 16:4-5), eleven to the sons of Korah (probably a

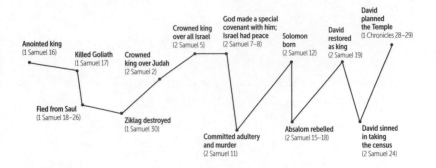

The Highs and Lows of David's Life

school of musicians unrelated to the rebel of Numbers 16–17), and two to Solomon. Ethan the Ezrahite (Psalm 89) and Heman the Ezrahite (Psalm 88) each wrote one (see 1 Kings 4:31).

The Psalms portray a broad range of human emotions: joy, pain, grief, doubt, and faith. Some of the psalms reflect specific historical events, while others have a broader and more timeless nature. Many give prophetic glimpses, especially of the coming Messiah.

Digging Into Psalms

A Psalm of David?

Evangelical scholars debate the origin of the superscriptions in the Psalms; but unlike the section headings in other books (which were provided by the translators), these superscriptions are present in all known texts, albeit with some variation between the Hebrew Masoretic Text and the Greek Septuagint. Of the 150 psalms, 116 have a superscription; seventy-three of those psalms bear the title "of David." The word *of* may indicate that David wrote the psalm, or that it is about him or for him. The biggest issue in attributing every "Psalm of David" to David is that some of them contain anachronisms, such as references to the Temple (which Solomon built after David's death). On the other hand, Jesus attributed some psalms to David personally, and his argument would not make sense if it referred to someone else (Mark 12:36-37). I tend to read the anachronisms in light of the Gospels and think that David sometimes wrote of the Temple prophetically, while at other times he referred to heaven as the temple (Hebrews 9:11). Godly people, committed to the authority of Scripture, disagree on this issue, and we should all remain humble.[1] Still, many references to David's life are tied deliberately to particular psalms. The highs and lows of his life (pictured at the beginning of this chapter) provide helpful context.

Structure

The Psalms are broken into five books, but no consensus exists about why each psalm appears in a particular book. Perhaps each book corresponds to one of the five books of the Law, but we have little specific evidence for this. Each book ends with a hymn of praise (a doxology), suggesting that once they may have circulated separately.

Though later scholars added chapter designations to make it easier for readers to locate specific passages, the numbering of the psalms comes from antiquity, with two exceptions: The Septuagint combines Psalm 9 and 10 and splits Psalm 147 into two psalms. Many technical commentaries reference Psalms 10–147 with two numbers, one for the Hebrew and English numbering and one for the Septuagint.

Special Concerns

Psalms were created to be sung, and like songs today, they employ stock metaphors and hyperbole to make their point. Because we have the Psalms in written form only, we do not know the meaning of some musical terms. The most common, *Selah*, probably refers to a pause, maybe for a musical interlude (the NLT translates it as "Interlude"). The wide variety of proposed translations for these terms should make us humble. Consider the various suggestions for *Miktam* in Psalm 16 and Psalms 56–60: "golden psalm," "silent prayer," and "indelible psalm."[2]

The Psalms use several stereotyped forms (see the introduction to the Writings for some of the main devices employed in Hebrew poetry). They use shared language and structure to reflect on a wide variety of situations, which makes the Psalms as well suited for worship now as when they were first written. The symbols lift their joys and struggles above immediate circumstances and make them applicable for every occasion.

Scholars often break down the Psalms by type. Below, I consider an example of each of five main categories of psalm, with some suggestions for interpreting other psalms of the same type.[3] Keep in mind that psalms can fall into more than one category.

Laments

Laments, the most common type of psalm, complain to God about some difficulty, either in a corporate (Psalm 44) or private (Psalm 69) setting. Laments follow a basic pattern:

- a cry to God for help;
- a stylized description of the problem;
- a confession of trust;
- a request for help;
- a promise to worship once the problem is resolved; and
- a confession of faith that God has heard.

The elements appear in different order and may add or skip some arguments (like a declaration of innocence).

Jesus quoted Psalm 22, an important individual lament, while on the cross (Matthew 27:46; Mark 15:34). It begins with a cry to God for help in the face of apparent abandonment (Psalm 22:1) and expresses faith that God truly saves (Psalm 22:2-5). Then it describes rejection, mockery, and abuse that has left the author hungry, thirsty, and stripped naked (Psalm 22:6-18; see Matthew 27:35-43; John 19:24-28). David cries out for mercy, describing the enemy as dogs, lions, and wild oxen (Psalm 22:19-21). Then he promises to praise God before the people (Psalm 22:22; see Hebrews 2:12) and moves into a lengthy assurance that the Lord will answer (Psalm 22:23-31).

The imprecatory psalm provides a particularly challenging type of lament, as the one praying it asks specifically for divine judgment. Psalm 137, one of the best known and most graphic examples, ends with verse 9: "Happy is the one who takes your babies and smashes them against the rocks!" How should Christians take these kinds of psalms that seem to contradict the call of Jesus to forgive our enemies? Bear in mind that God had already taught his people to forgive their enemies (Leviticus 19:17-18).

First, the imprecatory psalms accurately record how these people feel when they pour out their hearts to God in prayer. They ask the Lord to bring justice to an unjust situation (Deuteronomy 32:35; Romans 12:19; Hebrews 10:30). Second, the imprecatory psalms focus primarily on the enemies of God and God's people, more than on the personal enemies of the individual. Psalm 59 gives us an obvious example: As an individual, David refuses to lift a hand against Saul, but as the Lord's anointed, he prays that God will confound Saul's soldiers so that the nation will recognize God as their real king (Psalm 59:13). David can forgive David's enemies even while praying for God's wrath against the enemies of the King of Israel. In a similar way, a father may turn the other cheek to his personal enemies but defend his family, or a pastor may pray for God to stop those harming the church, as Paul did (Galatians 5:12). The Lord will judge the wicked, even though we personally forgive them and seek their salvation.

Thanksgiving and Praise Psalms

This category includes psalms that give thanks for a specific event (Psalm 66) and those that praise the Lord more generally (Psalm 148). Psalm 118 provides a good model of the basic pattern. It commits to give thanks (Psalm 118:1-4), summarizes the reason (Psalm 118:5-9), recalls the problem and God's rescue in more detail (Psalm 118:10-21), reflects on the character of God as revealed by his intervention (Psalm 118:22-28), and closes with another call to praise (Psalm 118:29). Like the laments, the problem is often described poetically, making it easily adaptable to a variety of situations. The reflection on God's character often offers rich theological significance, as in Psalm 118:22-23, which lays out the principle that God often chooses what people despise. Jesus applied those verses to himself in Matthew 21:42 (paralleled in Mark 12:10-11; Luke 20:17; Acts 4:11; 1 Peter 2:4-7).

Royal Psalms

The royal psalms reflect on the king's enthronement (Psalm 24) or God's blessings to the king (Psalm 110). They closely intertwine with the prophetic hope that one day the Lord himself will somehow rule through David's heir, a promise Jesus fulfills. When we consider wicked leaders of our day, we can remember that Israelites sang these songs during the reigns of evil kings such as Ahab, Manasseh, and Herod. Human rulers may fail us and our circumstances may seem out of control, but a coming King will rule in righteousness forever.

Psalm 2 gives us a good example of a royal psalm. It begins with a threat to the king (Psalm 2:1-3), promises God's deliverance (Psalm 2:4-6), reflects the king's trust in God (Psalm 2:7-9), and calls on the nations to serve the Lord and his Christ (Psalm 2:10-12). The New Testament frequently references this psalm. The Gospels often identify Jesus as the royal son (Matthew 3:17; Mark 1:11; Luke 3:22; Matthew 17:5; Mark 9:7; Luke 9:35; cf. Acts 13:33; Hebrews 1:5; 5:5). Acts 4:25-26 refers to the futile rebellion of the nations against him, while Revelation 11:18 and 19:19 allude to it. Hebrews 1:2 and Revelation 2:26-27; 12:5; 19:15 promise Jesus' certain victory.

Wisdom Psalms

Wisdom psalms give advice for a good life and lay out the general (but not unbreakable) principles of reward for goodness and punishment for sin. They feature a less stylized form than the previous types of psalms; Psalm 112 provides a good example. It begins with a call to praise the Lord, like a hymn of praise, but quickly moves into practical counsel for godly living, warning of the dangers of wickedness. Second Corinthians 9:9 quotes its straightforward teaching about the importance of generosity.

Psalms of Trust

Like the wisdom psalms, psalms of trust are diverse in form but united by their content. They all express certainty in God's help, despite the people's trials, and reflect on God's character. Psalm 16 describes God as David's refuge, his inheritance, and his cup of blessing. David stands unafraid even in the face of death, believing that God will not leave his body to decay. Peter recites a large portion of this psalm at Pentecost (Acts 2:25-28), explaining that David, who died and whose body decayed, had only partially fulfilled this psalm. The psalm ultimately referred to Jesus, who rose again. We can pray this psalm with special hope, knowing that our death will not be final; Jesus conquered death once and for all.

Living It Out

Authentic Worship: Modern worship services tend toward the upbeat; after all, our faith is founded on *good news*. But God inspired more psalms of lament than any other type of psalm. We do ourselves and our churches a disservice if we try to deny the reality of pain rather than handing it over to God for healing. The psalmists complain frankly to God about their situations, declare what they do not understand, and then rest in their trust of him. What better model of worship could we have?

Reflection: Psalms spends much time reflecting on the past, remembering who God is and what he has done. The psalmist often talks to himself; the very literal King James Version of Psalm 103:1 has inspired generations of songwriters: "Bless the LORD, O my soul: and all that is within me, *bless* his holy name." Dr. Martin Lloyd-Jones put it profoundly: "Have you realized that most of your unhappiness in life is due to the fact that you are listening to yourself instead of talking to yourself?"[4] Though many today understand meditation as emptying the mind, the biblical idea of meditation calls for us to deliberately reflect on God's Word (Psalm 1:2; 1 Timothy 4:15). The Psalms give us a remarkable tool for self-talk. The vivid word pictures of the past can express our feelings and then point us to the Lord as the answer.

Questions for Review

1. Should we use the superscriptions of the Psalms to interpret them? Why or why not?

2. What are the main types of psalms?

3. How can Christians use the Psalms in worship?

4. What is an imprecatory psalm? Why does the Bible include these kinds of psalms? Do they contradict the ethic of the New Testament?

18

Proverbs

Where there is charity and wisdom there is neither fear nor ignorance.
FRANCIS OF ASSISI

The Big Picture

Proverbs, a collection of wise sayings, describes the pattern typical of life. Each short proverb offers a memorable statement of a general truth, not an infallible promise or commandment. The brevity of proverbs means that they often lack nuance and must be understood in light of the rest of the Bible. The book took shape over a large portion of Israel's history, at least from Solomon to Hezekiah (about three hundred years) and possibly even longer. Most proverbs use parallelism (see the introduction to the Writings), presenting wise sayings in either contrasting or synonymous sets.

Digging Into Proverbs

Structure

1. Introduction (Proverbs 1:1-7)

2. The Heart of Wisdom (Proverbs 1:8–9:18)

3. Proverbs of Solomon (Proverbs 10:1–22:16)

4. Words of the Wise (Proverbs 22:17–24:34)

5. Hezekiah's Collection of Solomon's Proverbs
    (Proverbs 25–29)

6. Sayings of Agur (Proverbs 30)

7. Sayings of Lemuel (Proverbs 31)
    a. The Ideal King (Proverbs 31:1-9)
    b. The Ideal Wife (Proverbs 31:10-31)

Introduction (Proverbs 1:1-7)

The important opening of Proverbs attributes the bulk of the book to Solomon, known for his wise sayings (1 Kings 4:32), and explains the purpose of what follows. Proverbs trains the young and the simple to live well and helps the wise grow wiser. This gives us some insight into how to approach the book: On its most basic level, we can find memorable, helpful advice for how to live. But as we grow in wisdom, we should meditate on these brief statements to understand them more fully. Verse 7 has particular

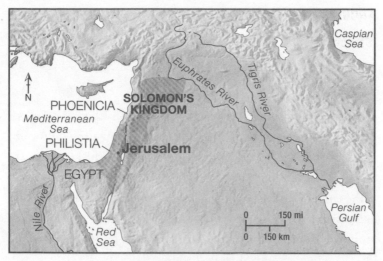

Solomon's Kingdom

importance: "Fear of the LORD is the foundation of true knowledge, but fools despise wisdom and discipline." This very practical book only rarely gets theological, but it presupposes a world ruled by a righteous God who has revealed himself to his people (Proverbs 2:5-8; 9:10; 16:1-9, 33).

The Heart of Wisdom (Proverbs 1:8-9:18)

This section differs from the others. Rather than short, mostly disconnected sayings, it presents a lengthy argument for the importance of wisdom. It personifies wisdom as a woman crying out to people to come and know her. Wisdom is not reserved for the select few, but she cries in the streets for anyone willing to come out and learn (Proverbs 8:1-11; 9:1-6). Solomon warns about the other voices that try to distract us: the greedy (Proverbs 1:19; 15:27; 21:26; 28:22, 25); the sexually immoral (Proverbs 2:16-19; 5:1-23; 6:24-35); the proud (Proverbs 16:5; 21:4, 24; 30:13, 32);

and the violent (Proverbs 3:31-32; 6:16-19). Following those voices leads to death (Proverbs 9:13-18), but following wisdom leads to life and prosperity (Proverbs 9:11-12).

Proverbs of Solomon (Proverbs 10:1-22:16)

Most of the proverbs in this section feature antithetical couplets, presenting two paths and their respective destinations. Proverbs 10:27 provides a representative example: "Fear of the LORD lengthens one's life, but the years of the wicked are cut short." Like Moses at the end of Deuteronomy, or Jesus in the Sermon on the Mount, Solomon pleads with us to choose life. Some of the warnings seem mundane (don't cosign for a loan, Proverbs 11:15), and some are life-changing (standing before the king, Proverbs 20:2).

Words of the Wise (Proverbs 22:17-24:34)

These proverbs, called "the words of the wise," are not attributed to any particular person. They represent an ancient tradition, probably with roots outside of Israel.[1] While God's common grace makes the basic principles for life available to everyone, the inspired authors present to us the insight of the Lord.

Hezekiah's Collection of Solomon's Proverbs (Proverbs 25-29)

This selection, somewhat more organized than the earlier proverbs of Solomon, puts the proverbs in groups by topic. Laziness, for example, provides the theme of Proverbs 26:12-16, and the proverbs in 27:23-27 all focus on financial prudence.

Sayings of Agur (Proverbs 30)

The name Agur does not appear in the Old Testament outside of Proverbs 30:1, and many scholars think that he and Lemuel may have been Gentiles. Others see these as pseudonyms for Solomon.

If Agur were a Gentile, he was a godly one who references the Lord frequently in verses 1-9. Most of this chapter consists of lists that model wisdom or folly (as in Proverbs 30:24-28).

Sayings of Lemuel (Proverbs 31)
The unknown King Lemuel draws his proverbs from his mother's teaching, making it one of the few passages in the Bible originating with a woman. It begins with a discussion of a godly leader and then describes the ideal wife (Proverbs 31:10-31).

Living It Out
Sexual Purity: Many today consider any discussion of sexual morality out of touch. Our culture cannot accept that God created sex to picture how a husband and wife become one (Matthew 19:5-6; 1 Corinthians 6:16). But sex is never casual and unimportant; it affects us on the deepest level. Solomon's marriages to idolatrous women influenced him much more deeply than friends ever could.

Warnings against adulterous women seem especially offensive today, and some might shrink from acknowledging these texts. But notice that Solomon spreads the blame around. He calls both the man and the woman wicked fools. The New Testament, as usual, doesn't merely repeat this theme (Hebrews 13:4), but intensifies it. Sex outside of marriage doesn't make guilty individuals merely fools; it makes them blasphemers. Marriage gives us a picture of Christ's relationship with the church, and so marriage should remain as holy as what it represents (Ephesians 5:22-32; Revelation 19:7). We are God's temple, and joining his temple with immorality brings disgrace (1 Corinthians 6:15-17).

Wisdom: See 1 and 2 Kings: Living It Out.

Questions for Review

1. What is a proverb?

2. Compare and contrast Proverbs with Job. What would we be missing if we did not have both?

3. Why are marriage, family, and sexual morality mentioned so frequently?

4. How do the references to money and wealth set the boundaries on our priorities and our behavior?

19

Job

Be patient. Our Playwright may show
In some fifth Act what this wild Drama means.
ALFRED TENNYSON
"The Play"

The Big Picture

This book tells the story of Job's struggle to understand why the righteous suffer. After an opening scene in the heavenly court, Job loses his wealth, family, and health. His friends come to visit, and in a series of speeches suggest Job himself must somehow be to blame. Job expresses his doubts without losing his faith. Finally, God answers and demonstrates that Job lacks the ability to either understand or judge his plans. Job repents and is restored. We will not understand many mysteries of life on this side of eternity, but we can trust in God, who does.

Job fits into the genre of wisdom literature poetry. While Proverbs shows how life normally works, where the hardworking and the righteous prosper, Job deals with life on the margins, examining how we should think about times that fall outside the pattern. Job shows us that even the faithful and the godly can struggle to understand God's will, but ultimately, we must trust the Lord's heart even when we do not know his reasons. We do not know either the author or the date of the book, but some verbal clues suggest the work's great antiquity. The presence of a worshiper of the Lord in the land of Uz, who makes sacrifices without a priest, has led many commentators to believe the events recounted in Job take place during the time of Abraham. If that is true, Job may be the oldest book in the Bible.

Digging Into Job

Structure

Job features a series of speeches, with narrative bookends on either side. The climax, after all Job's foolish friends finish speaking, comes in the dialogue between Job and God himself.

1. Prologue (Job 1–2)

2. Opening Dialogues (Job 3–27)
   a. Job's Complaint (Job 3)
   b. Eliphaz and Job (Job 4–7; 15–17; 22–24)
   c. Bildad and Job (Job 8–10; 18–19; 25–27)
   d. Zophar and Job (Job 11–14; 20–21)

3. Monologues (Job 28–37)
   a. Job's Defense (Job 28–31)
   b. Elihu (Job 32–37)

4. Final Dialogue (Job 38:1–42:6)
   a. God Speaks (Job 38–41:34)
   b. Job's Responses to the Lord (Job 40:3-5; 42:1-6)

5. Epilogue (Job 42:7-17)

Prologue (Job 1-2)
The book opens with a description of Job as a blessed and righteous man, but quickly pivots to the heavenly court, where Satan claims Job acts righteously only because of his pleasant circumstances. God allows Satan to remove Job's blessings one by one, leaving him childless, poor, and sick, with only an embittered wife to comfort him.

Opening Dialogues (Job 3-27)
At the center of the book, Job's three friends accuse Job and Job responds. They speak in the same order each time—Eliphaz, Bildad, and Zophar—and go through three cycles of dialogue (although Zophar does not participate in the third round). Each of Job's friends holds a simplistic position that everyone gets what they deserve and that suffering is proof of sin. When Job defends himself, sometimes his language seems blasphemous (Job 7:11-21), but it comes from a place of faith (Job 13:15). Each cycle grows a little crueler than the one before it, and Job's responses grow increasingly bitter.

Monologues (Job 28-37)
In chapter 28, Job gives a discourse on wisdom, in which he continues to affirm that worshiping God always remains at the center of true wisdom (Job 28:28). Job lays out his case in detail, claiming

his innocence, and asks why God has allowed him to sink so low. When he finishes, he goes silent (Job 31:40).

The next monologue comes from Elihu, a previously unmentioned young man. This angry young man takes Job to task for putting his own righteousness before God's. Yet his final failure to understand God's ways or to answer Job shows that the Lord's wisdom confounds the wise of every generation.

Final Dialogue (Job 38:1–42:6)

At last, the Lord himself responds—but not how we might expect. The Lord does not tell Job about the prologue or explain spiritual warfare. Instead, God effectively asks Job, "Who do you think you are?" Where was Job when the Lord built the earth (Job 38:4-7)? Could Job control the stars (Job 38:31)? How could Job criticize God when Job does not even understand the fundamental order of the world (Job 40:2)? Job humbly agrees with God (Job 40:3-5), and God begins his second speech. Its similar content emphasizes Job's inability to rule over creation (Job 40:9–41:34).

If God had answered Job by describing the heavenly scene of the opening chapters, the book would do us little good. But the Lord's response is both far more helpful and far more humbling: Job, like us, could not understand even if God had explained everything (Job 42:3).

Epilogue (Job 42:7-17)

In the narrative conclusion to the book, the Lord rebukes Job's three friends for their arrogance and vindicates Job. (He does not address Elihu.) The friends must repent, and Job must intercede for them so they can be forgiven (Job 42:8-9). In the end, Job is given twice as much wealth as he had before, ten more children, and a long life (Job 42:12-16). The reward for his righteousness

The Land of Uz?

We do not know the exact location of Job's home of Uz, but some traditions (including Josephus) place it in the region of Bashan, in the western part of modern Syria (the northeastern part of the map above). Other scholars place it closer to Mount Seir (the southernmost part of the map).

reaffirms the general pattern of wisdom literature—namely, that God rewards good and punishes evil—but the book leaves much room for the incomprehensible sovereignty of God in working out life's details.

Living It Out

Satan: The Old Testament only rarely describes Satan, literally "the accuser," and he plays an important role in Job only at the very beginning before he recedes into the background. We can make several observations from the way the book portrays Satan, each of which other Scriptures verify.

First, Satan is an accuser. He immediately lives up to his title, challenging Job's standing before God (Zechariah 3:1-2; Revelation 12:10). Second, Satan is an angelic being who comes before God at the same time as the other sons of God (2 Corinthians 11:14). Third, Satan must obey God; the two are not equals. Although some imagine a dualistic world in which God and Satan war against each other with equal powers, in fact, Satan can do nothing to Job or to anyone else without divine permission (Luke 22:31). Finally, Satan is a tempter who tries to entice people to sin (Matthew 4:1-11; 1 Thessalonians 3:5). Job's faith in God's righteousness and his own personal integrity allowed him to resist the temptation he faced, and Revelation 12:10-11 presents the same path to us.

Suffering: In the Hebrew canon, Job fittingly follows Proverbs. Though wisdom usually leads to a better life and wickedness usually leads to suffering, sometimes the righteous suffer too. The theologian's pat answer that "only one righteous man ever suffered, and he volunteered" is true insofar as it goes; in fact, no one but Jesus gets worse than they deserve. But such an answer is far too simple. We must recognize that even the approximate justice of this world sometimes falls short. Sometimes suffering directly corrects some sin in our lives. Sometimes suffering gives us a chance to display God's power. Suffering might prepare us for some challenge we do not know we will face, or serve some onlooker we don't even know. We cannot always understand the purpose of our suffering, but we can trust the one who works all things together for good (Romans 8:28).

20

Five Festal Scrolls

I need Thee ev'ry hour,
In joy or pain;
Come quickly and abide,
Or life is vain.
ANNIE S. HAWKS
"I Need Thee Every Hour"

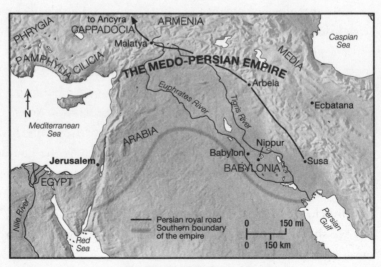

The World of Esther's Day

The Big Picture

Each of these books, called *Megilloth* (Hebrew for "scrolls") in the Jewish canon, is traditionally read in conjunction with a holy day. These diverse books each represent an emotional extreme of either joy or pain and show God's sovereignty in both.

Digging Into the Five Festal Scrolls

Song of Songs

Sometimes called Song of Solomon or Canticles (from the Latin for "song"), this love poem explores the relationship between a husband and wife and traditionally was read on Passover. Though Song of Songs is often attributed to Solomon, someone else may have written it in his honor (see "A Psalm of David?" in the chapter on Psalms). For the linguistic arguments made against Solomon's authorship, see Ecclesiastes below.

This anthology of poems does not develop smoothly, like a straightforward narrative. The writer tells the story from several perspectives: the shepherd-king, the woman, the woman's brothers, and the other young women of Jerusalem. Modern readers often find the agricultural metaphors of the book disconcerting, but each compares the beloved to the most splendid things imaginable. The collection of poems fits within the canon of Scripture to remind us that God gives us the good gifts of marriage and love. Song of Songs primarily concerns literal romantic love. Because all marriages picture Christ and the church, we can make that connection in a secondary sense, but we should never allow it to overshadow the book's plain meaning (Ephesians 5:32).

Ruth

Ruth gives us a delightful spark of light during the dark period of Judges. During a famine, seen as a divine judgment during a period of wickedness, God carefully arranges the pieces of history. Ruth, a Moabite woman who marries one of Naomi's sons, demonstrates her integrity and character by voluntarily coming to Bethlehem to live with Naomi and serving the God of Israel. Her integrity catches the eye of Boaz, a generous businessman who eventually redeems her. The two marry, and she becomes pregnant and has a son, the grandfather of David. The book explains King David's scandalous Moabite heritage as part of the Lord's gracious deliverance, shows God's sovereignty over both Israel and the nations, and foreshadows how Jesus, the son of David, will bring salvation to the Gentiles. Each chapter forms an act in this short story.

1. The Problem: Death of Naomi's Sons (Ruth 1)

2. The Hope: Ruth in Boaz's Field (Ruth 2)

3. The Solution: Boaz the Kinsman-Redeemer (Ruth 3)

4. The Happy Ending: The Redemption and the Heir (Ruth 4)

Lamentations

Lamentations reflects tragically on God's judgment of Jerusalem and its destruction by the Babylonians. Early and consistent tradition attributes Lamentations to Jeremiah the prophet, and few reasons exist to question the consensus. The book has an emotional intensity expected from an eyewitness. It probably dates from soon after the fall of Jerusalem in 586 BC; it was read annually on the anniversary of that defeat. Its five poems are structured around the twenty-two letters of the Hebrew alphabet. Its acrostic structure suggests comprehensive grief ("from A to Z"), much like Psalm 119 praises God's Word as fully meeting every human need. In the uniquely structured chapter 3, each letter repeats three times (similar to English poems with lines beginning AAA BBB CCC, etc.). The twenty-two verses of chapter 5 are not arranged as an acrostic. The book's emphasis on the middle chapter, and the collapse of the common structure in the final chapter, support the idea that Lamentations is written as a chiasm, where chapter 1 corresponds to chapter 5, chapter 2 corresponds to chapter 4, and chapter 3 represents the climax and turning point.

1. Sorrow at Jerusalem's Judgment (Lamentations 1)

2. God's Anger at Israel's Sin (Lamentations 2)

3. God's Faithfulness (Lamentations 3)

4. God's Anger Satisfied (Lamentations 4)

5. Hope for Jerusalem's Restoration (Lamentations 5)

Ecclesiastes

Ecclesiastes, traditionally read during the Feast of Tabernacles, describes the futility of life "under the sun." Most understood Solomon to be its author (dated around 930 BC) because of the opening verse: "These are the words of the Teacher, King David's son, who ruled in Jerusalem." Of course, "King David's son" sometimes refers to a later heir (Matthew 1:20), but the king most associated with wisdom is Solomon (1 Kings 3:11-12). Two lines of evidence work against viewing Solomon as the author. First, the book uses both Persian and Aramaic words, out of place in the time of Solomon. Second, at least some passages seem to separate the author from the royal throne (Ecclesiastes 5:9; 10:20). Many scholars, including conservative ones, view the "David's son" language as a literary fiction, not intended to deceive the audience but to emphasize that futility affects all levels of life. Because of this, many commentaries simply refer to the author of the book as Qohelet or Kohelet (a transliteration of the Hebrew word translated *teacher* in the NLT).

The arguments against Solomonic authorship are not as strong as some suggest. We cannot fully detect Persian influences, and with the breadth of his empire's commerce, Solomon could have been influenced by the Aramaic language. In fact, no matter what time period is suggested for the book, it uses odd language. Which sounds stranger, a separation between the author and his throne or the author describing himself as a king?[1]

The somber book of Ecclesiastes repeatedly says, "everything is meaningless" (Ecclesiastes 1:2, 14; 2:1, 11; 12:8). It describes life's futility "under the sun," where everything we accomplish gets undone by time and chance. It offers a glimmer of hope at the end, when the author's eye shifts to the one who rules over the sun. All of us ought to fear God and obey him, knowing that he will judge us for everything in our lives (Ecclesiastes 12:13-14). The final judgment means everything is *not* a meaningless cycle after all. Everything works toward an end that makes sense only in light of the Lord. Life on earth for its own sake will never give us satisfaction or peace. As many outlines of Ecclesiastes exist as outliners, but the basic structure looks something like this:

1. Looking for Meaning Under the Sun (Ecclesiastes 1–3)

2. Failed Attempts to Find Meaning (Ecclesiastes 4–6)

3. Wisdom in Pursuit of Meaning (Ecclesiastes 7:1–12:8)

4. The Better Way (Ecclesiastes 12:9-14)

Esther

Esther, the story of the queen who rescues her people, is read at Purim, the holiday celebrating the events described in the book (*purim* is the Hebrew word for "lots," see Esther 3:7). It had to be written after the reign of Xerxes (the king in the book, who died in 465 BC) and probably before Alexander the Great's cultural hegemony (around 332 BC; the book's language betrays no evidence of Greek influence). We cannot narrow the date further, and we have no good evidence about the author's identity.

Esther does not explicitly mention God, Abraham, the covenant, or the Temple. The book feels almost like a secular account of how bravery and creativity prevent the genocide of the Israelites. Of course, the "coincidences" described in the book are not coincidences at all. Even though the book does not mention the battle of Thermopylae—in which a small band of Greeks delayed a much larger force of Persians from invading mainland Greece—it appears to shape the king's harsh treatment of Vashti in the first chapter. The hand of the Lord guides even two pagan armies to accomplish his plans.

The straightforward narrative tells how a Hebrew woman named Hadassah hides her ancestry and becomes the queen of Persia under the name Esther. A royal official, Haman, hates

Jews in general and Mordecai in particular, and plots to kill them all. Haman does not know that Mordecai is Esther's uncle and guardian, and all Haman's plans backfire. By the end of the story, Haman lies dead while Mordecai and Esther receive great honor.

The book of Esther, surprisingly, often uses humor. Irony drives the plot as God consistently reverses the plans of sinful people. Xerxes's pride opens the door for Esther to become queen. Haman gives the king advice on how to honor Mordecai (Esther 6:4-14), and Haman eventually dies on the gallows he intended for Mordecai (Esther 7:8-10). The attack on the Jews turns into a legally sanctioned slaughter of their enemies (Esther 9:5-17).

Living It Out

Providence: The books of Ruth and Esther remind us that in God's world there are no accidents of history. Though God is never mentioned in the book of Esther, and though Ruth was from Moab and not even an Israelite, God clearly orchestrates the events in their lives to protect his people and fulfill his promises.

In our modern world, people love to draw bold lines between the sacred and the secular. They may say, "Your religious convictions may belong in your church and your home (although maybe you shouldn't teach your children that they are *true*) but have no place in the public square." The Bible adamantly opposes any such reasoning. God created everything, and no sphere of life exists where he is not active. He expects his people to obey him always and everywhere.

Emotions: Song of Songs and Ecclesiastes showcase the broad range of human experience. From the ecstasy and newness of romantic love to the apparent collapse of meaning in death, the Bible never denies these feelings or calls on believers to smother them. Rather, it invites us to see them through a Christian worldview. Worshiping the God who is over the sun puts into perspective the futility of life under the sun, and we must understand the joys of marriage as gifts of a loving God. Even Lamentations, a dirge over Jerusalem's lost splendor, gives us permission to pour out our hearts in grief over God's actions in history, while we continue to trust, as Abraham did, that "the Judge of all the earth" will always "do what is right" (Genesis 18:25).

Questions for Review

1. How do Song of Songs and Ecclesiastes balance one another?

2. What is unusual about Esther? How does what is missing from the book contribute to the message of the book?

3. List the holidays associated with each of the Five Festal Scrolls and explain the connections.

21

Daniel

[Jesus] was not a slave to fortune but the King of history.

ANDREW PATERSON

Opening up John's Gospel

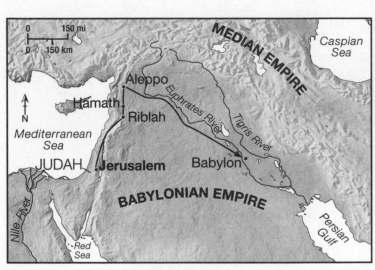

Taken to Babylon

The Big Picture

The prophet Daniel had the most globally focused message of all the prophets, focusing on the future of both Israel and the major Gentile powers. The book belongs to a genre called *apocalyptic literature*, which combines history with symbol-laden descriptions of the future. It was written between 605 BC (Daniel 1:1) and 536 BC (Daniel 10:1), the full time of the exile. Some scholars date the book to the second century BC, claiming that someone used Daniel as a pen name.[1] But Jesus himself attributed the book to Daniel (Matthew 24:15). Despite the brevity of the book of Daniel, the New Testament alludes to it more than seventy times.[2]

Digging Into Daniel

Structure

1. Historical Background (Daniel 1–6)
   a. Hebrews in the Palace (Daniel 1)
   b. Nebuchadnezzar's Dream (Daniel 2)
   c. The Fiery Furnace (Daniel 3)
   d. Nebuchadnezzar's Second Dream (Daniel 4)
   e. The Writing on the Wall (Daniel 5)
   f. Daniel in the Lion's Den (Daniel 6)

2. Visions of the Future (Daniel 7–12)
   a. Four Beasts (Daniel 7)
   b. Two Kingdoms (Daniel 8)
   c. Seventy Sets of Seven (Daniel 9)
   d. Coming Kings (Daniel 10–11)
   e. The End (Daniel 12)

Historical Background (Daniel 1-6)

The opening chapters contain some of the best-known stories in the Bible. Daniel and his three friends, all young men taken to Babylon in 605 BC, are brought to serve Nebuchadnezzar (see the map at the beginning of the chapter). Repeatedly, they must decide whether to remain faithful to God or surrender to the pressures of their new culture. In their diet (Daniel 1), their worship (Daniel 3), and Daniel's prayers (Daniel 6), they refuse to compromise, even when their integrity endangers their lives. When Shadrach, Meshach, and Abednego refuse to bow to an idol, Nebuchadnezzar throws them into a burning furnace. To his surprise, God protects them and a fourth man appears in the fire with them, someone Nebuchadnezzar says looks like "a son of the gods"—a delightfully ambiguous Aramaic phrase that could be understood as a pagan god, an angel, or a Son of God ("gods" is often translated as "God" in the Old Testament).[3] Nebuchadnezzar means it as a reference to one of many deities, but like Caiaphas in John 11:50-51, he speaks better than he knows.

This example illustrates the pattern of each temptation: someone challenges a believer's obedience to God, the believer chooses faith, God protects him, and the Gentiles glorify God. If the nation had followed this pattern, the exile never would have occurred. In chapters 2, 4, and 5, Daniel takes on a role reminiscent of Joseph in Egypt. He interprets mysteries for pagan rulers, becomes their trusted advisor, and through his service they recognize the power and wisdom of his God. Even in Babylon, the place of exile, God remains in control.

Visions of the Future (Daniel 7-12)

These complex visions have stirred controversy. We cannot possibly explain and evaluate every point of view, so I will offer my understanding of them, with the caveat that many wise and godly people disagree with me.

The vision in chapter 7 describes four beasts representing four world powers: Babylonia, Medo-Persia, Greece, and Rome. In chapter 9, Daniel receives a prophecy of seventy sets of seven that outline the future of Israel, from the time of the order to rebuild Jerusalem to the time of the end. While Jeremiah had predicted seventy years of exile, Daniel prophesies that it will take seventy sets of seven to remove the people's sin once and for all. If each of these "sevens" represents seven years, the prophecy points to 490 years.

The order to rebuild Jerusalem came in about 458 BC. Daniel predicted that after sixty-nine sets of seven, the Anointed One (the Christ) would come, be killed, and Jerusalem and the Temple would be destroyed once more (Daniel 9:25-26). Four hundred eighty-three years after 458 BC is AD 26, which brings us to the time of Christ's baptism and public ministry. Jesus was killed after a ministry of about three years, and the Romans destroyed Jerusalem in AD 70. But Daniel predicts a final king of the Romans, far greater than his predecessors, who will try to change God's law and set up an "abomination of desolation" in the Temple (Daniel 7:23-25; 8:23; 9:27; 11:31; 12:11). Some have tied this prophecy to Antiochus Epiphanes, who desecrated the sanctuary in 167 BC, but according to Jesus, the event has yet to happen (Matthew 24:15). Second Thessalonians 2:4 seems to say that this abomination of desolation will happen when a future king will go into the Temple and claim to be God. So apparently the 490-year clock stopped when Jesus began his ministry and will resume in the future for a final seven years.

That final seven-year period is usually called the Tribulation. God's people will suffer for "a time, times and half a time" (three and a half years) before the final rescue (Daniel 7:25-28; 12:7), when God will raise the dead, judge the wicked, and set up his Kingdom forever.

Living It Out

King of Kings: Nebuchadnezzar was called a "king of kings" (Ezekiel 26:7; Daniel 2:37) because his empire had swallowed up his enemies. But as soon as Daniel calls Nebuchadnezzar "the greatest of kings (Daniel 2:37), he also explains that the God of heaven gave the king his domain. The Lord raises up and removes kings (Daniel 2:21) and rules over all the kingdoms of the world (Daniel 4:17; 7:14). Daniel reminds us that only one Lord rules history, and the political games that seem so important now will be made irrelevant when the Son of Man sets up his Kingdom to rule with his people (Revelation 11:15). Because Daniel and his friends never forget who is really in control, they can live obedient and peaceful lives in the midst of pagan Babylon (Revelation 19:6).

Questions for Review

1. To which genre does the book of Daniel belong? How does that genre shape our interpretation of the book's content?

2. What is the main theme of the first six chapters? The last six?

3. How does Daniel demonstrate God's sovereignty in both the near and distant future? What are some practical ways that God's help in our past can reassure us of his care in our future?

22

Ezra and Nehemiah

Glorious things of thee are spoken,
Zion, city of our God;
he whose word cannot be broken
formed thee for his own abode;
on the Rock of Ages founded,
what can shake thy sure repose?
With salvation's walls surrounded,
thou may'st smile at all thy foes.

JOHN NEWTON
"Glorious Things of Thee Are Spoken"

The Big Picture

Ezra and Nehemiah present the final chapters of Old Testament history and originally were read as one book. Ezra has traditionally been viewed as the author of Ezra, Nehemiah, and Chronicles, making liberal use of earlier sources (including the personal memoirs of Nehemiah). Many modern scholars agree that all these books came from the pen of one person but doubt that Ezra wrote them. In either case, the book was finalized by about 400 BC.

Ezra and Nehemiah describe the first wave of the return to Canaan (in 538 BC) and the second (led by Ezra in 458 BC), overlapping with the prophets Haggai and Zechariah. The book of Ezra features no overt miracles, but the hand of the Lord unmistakably fulfills his word (Isaiah 44:28; Jeremiah 29:10-14). Ezra and Nehemiah lead the people in both physical renewal (rebuilding the Temple and the walls) and spiritual renewal (breaking off their marriages to pagans and reaffirming the Law). In some ways, they form the mirror image of the political and religious breakdown at the end of Judges, restoring what had failed both back then and many times since.

Digging Into Ezra and Nehemiah

Structure

1. First Return (Ezra 1–2)

2. Rebuilding the Temple (Ezra 3–6)

3. Second Return (Ezra 7–8)

4. Rebuilding the People (Ezra 9–10)

5. Nehemiah's Return (Nehemiah 1–2)

6. Walls Rebuilt (Nehemiah 3–7)

7. Covenant Renewed (Nehemiah 8–10)

8. Resettlement and Reformation (Nehemiah 11–13)

Ezra

Ezra's first six chapters describe the first wave of exiles returning to Israel under Zerubbabel, the heir of Jehoiachin, during the ministries of Haggai and Zechariah. During this time, Jeshua and Zerubbabel oversee the reconstruction of the altar and the Temple (Ezra 3). The Samaritans (Ezra 4:1-2) want to help reconstruct the Temple, but the Jewish leaders refuse to let anyone participate who is not faithful exclusively to the Lord. Their opponents convince the king to delay the rebuilding of the Temple, but no one can stop what God has started (Ezra 4:23-24). King Darius approves the reconstruction of the Temple and even finances it, so the Temple is finally finished (Ezra 6).

Ezra 7 begins much later, when the priest returns to Jerusalem. He devotes himself to the law of Moses and teaches it to the people (Ezra 7:10). Some of God's people, even some of the priests, have intermarried with the Gentiles and have "taken up the detestable practices" of the pagans (Ezra 9:1-2). Ezra pours his heart out to God in a powerful prayer in which he repents of the sins of his people (Ezra 9:5-15; cf. Isaiah 6:5; Daniel 9). He then calls on the Israelites to divorce their foreign wives and they do, rededicating themselves to God (Ezra 10).

Nehemiah

Nehemiah, cupbearer to the Persian king, feels grieved when he hears that Jerusalem's walls have not been rebuilt. He prays for the chance to go and rebuild them, which God graciously allows (Nehemiah 1–2). Like Ezra, Nehemiah faces opposition (Nehemiah 2:19; 4:1-15) but gets to work anyway. Nehemiah understands that God frustrates the plans of Israel's enemies not by sending fire from heaven, but by encouraging the hearts of his people (Nehemiah 4:15, 20; 6:16). Meanwhile, Nehemiah calls the

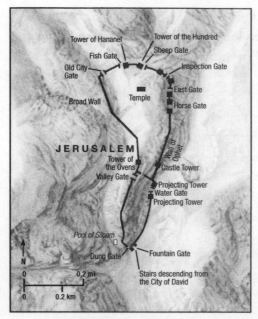

Restoring the City Walls

people to repent of their mistreatment of one another (Nehemiah 5), blending the physical and spiritual work of rebuilding Jerusalem. Their enemies hire a false prophet to discourage them, but the wall still gets completed in just fifty-two days (Nehemiah 6).

With the people settled and the walls rebuilt, Ezra reads the law of Moses to the remnant and explains it, passage by passage (Nehemiah 8:8). When the people understand their sin and God's standard, they weep in grief, but Ezra and Nehemiah encourage them instead to celebrate the return of the Law (Nehemiah 8:10). Just as when Josiah rediscovered the Law and renewed the Passover (2 Kings 23), so this generation turns back to God and renews the Festival of Shelters (Nehemiah 8:13-18). The people confess their sins and renew the covenant (Nehemiah 9–10).

After this, people are selected by lot to resettle Jerusalem (Nehemiah 11). The wall is dedicated and provisions for the Temple are made. Nehemiah 13 ends on a bittersweet note. Many of the sins addressed earlier in the book have resurfaced, and Nehemiah must deal with them again. So here, at the end of Old Testament history, the same problems resurface. Although the people renewed the old covenant, they did not have the new covenant written on their hearts. Ezra—Nehemiah feels encouraging, but also leaves readers longing for another Priest and King who can get to the heart of the problem, once and for all.

Living It Out

Leadership: Amazingly, more godly leaders (Haggai, Zechariah, Ezra, Nehemiah, Jeshua, Sheshbazzar, and Zerubbabel) appear in this brief period than the total number of righteous kings of Judah. Jeremiah had written about a time when the Lord would give them righteous leaders again (Jeremiah 3:15), and finally they get a taste (ultimately fulfilled by Jesus; cf. Ezekiel 34:23). These leaders serve and love the people, but they love the Lord more and are faithful to him regardless of the cost. Imagine what would happen if we had more such leaders today. May God send us godly leaders, both in the spiritual sphere (1 Timothy 3:1-9; Titus 1:6-9) and in the political one (Proverbs 16:12). May we *be* godly leaders, willing to say and do the hard things, for God's glory.

Marriage: At this pivotal time, and under the Old Testament Law, Ezra and Nehemiah make the Israelites divorce their foreign wives, lest they be led into idolatry like Solomon. In the New Testament, believers are told not to divorce their unbelieving spouses, in hopes that they might win the unbelievers to Christ (1 Corinthians 7:12-16). But that doesn't mean the choice of spouse doesn't matter. Our mate has more influence on us, for good or bad, than any other human being. In 1 Corinthians 7:39, Paul places just one restriction on who Christians can marry: they must wed other believers *only*. True compatibility is not about race, class, or personality quiz type, but about a common faith. If you have married an unbeliever, and the person is willing to stay in the marriage, the harsh standard of Ezra and Nehemiah does not apply to you (since we live in a different era). But if you have yet to marry, this story should make you think *very* carefully about whom you decide to marry.

Questions for Review

1. Why does Nehemiah end by addressing some of the same sins that he had already confronted? What tension exists at the end of this book?

2. Why did Ezra make the people divorce their pagan wives? How should Christians think about marriage today?

3. What role did Ezra and Nehemiah each play in the restoration of the Israelites?

23

1 and 2 Chronicles

God must be at the center of you and everything you do.
Because when God is at the center,
you are able to experience balance and focus.

JOHN RAINES
"God at the Center"

The Big Picture

Chronicles, at the end of the Hebrew canon, retells the history of 1 Samuel—2 Kings, but with a more hopeful perspective. The Chronicler (traditionally Ezra, see Ezra—Nehemiah) wrote after the return from exile, sometime around 450–400 BC. Unlike Samuel and Kings, written during the nation's decline to call the people to repentance as the exile drew near, Chronicles looks back in worship at the hand of God through all the nation's trials. I will not recount all the history summarized in the chapters on Samuel and Kings but will instead emphasize the unique features of Chronicles and its special place in the canon.

Digging Into 1 and 2 Chronicles

Structure

1. Genealogies (1 Chronicles 1–9)

2. King David (1 Chronicles 10–29)
   a. David's Rise (1 Chronicles 10–12)
   b. David's Reign (1 Chronicles 13–22)
   c. David's Dynasty (1 Chronicles 23–29)

3. King Solomon (2 Chronicles 1–9)
   a. Solomon's Wisdom (2 Chronicles 1)
   b. Solomon's Temple (2 Chronicles 2–7)
   b. Solomon's Wealth (2 Chronicles 8–9)

4. Kings of Judah (2 Chronicles 10–36)
   a. Rehoboam and Abijah: Wicked
      (2 Chronicles 10–13)
   b. Asa and Jehoshaphat: Some Good
      (2 Chronicles 14:1–21:3)
   c. Jehoram, Ahaziah, and Athaliah: Wicked
      (2 Chronicles 21:4–22:12)
   d. Joash, Amaziah, and Uzziah: Some Good
      (2 Chronicles 23–26)
   e. Jotham: Righteous (2 Chronicles 27)
   f. Ahaz: Wicked (2 Chronicles 28)
   g. Hezekiah: Righteous (2 Chronicles 29–32)
   h. Manasseh and Amon: Wicked (2 Chronicles 33)
   i. Josiah: Righteous (2 Chronicles 34–35)

    j. Jehoahaz, Jehoiakim, Jehoiachin, and Zedekiah:
        Wicked (2 Chronicles 36:1-16)

    k. Exile and Return (2 Chronicles 36:17-23)

Genealogies (1 Chronicles 1-9)

Lengthy genealogies do not mean much to many modern Western readers, but the Chronicles see them as essential. These opening chapters serve at least three purposes.

First, before outlining the history of Israel, the author demonstrates that the same God has been at work since the beginning. Second, he provides a pedigree for a people who have lost their homes and who are in danger of losing their identity. They must not forget that they are children of Abraham, Isaac, and Jacob. Third, by going back to Adam, he reminds his readers that God is the Lord of all the earth, including Persia and Babylon. God has brought them back to the land, and even though he has not yet fulfilled all of his promises, he will do so.

King David (1 Chronicles 10-29)

Chronicles all but skips over Saul so that it can focus on King David (David and Solomon's combined seventy-three years of reign get more attention than the remaining 345 years of Judah). Saul does, however, serve as a model for the sin of the whole nation. When they turn from God, the Lord rejects them and withdraws their blessings. God sends a new king instead, one who will follow him and lead the people to him. Of course, Saul also provides a picture of the world. All of us have turned from God to sin (Romans 1), but God has sent a new King to make things right again.

King Solomon (2 Chronicles 1–9)

The most remarkable thing about Chronicles' description of Solomon's reign is not what it includes, but what it doesn't. It never even mentions Solomon's idolatry late in life, but instead emphasizes the details of the Temple, Solomon's greatest achievement. Yet, even in his dedication prayer (2 Chronicles 6), Solomon confesses the inadequacy of the Temple to hold God. When the people turn to the Temple and pray, the Lord will hear "from heaven." This reminds readers that God's real throne has never been shaken, regardless of the destruction and reconstruction of the Jerusalem Temple.

Kings of Judah (2 Chronicles 10–36)

Chronicles addresses the northern kings only tangentially, focusing instead on the remnant of Judah who have returned to the land. When Judah remains righteous, the site of the Temple and the tribe of the King will bring blessing to the whole nation, as

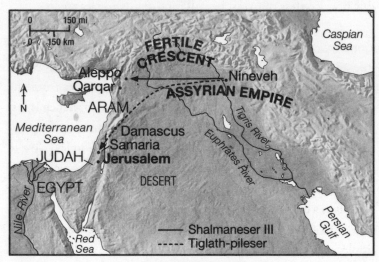

The Assyrian Empire

surely as God has designed Israel to bring blessing to the whole world. Chronicles, unlike 2 Kings, reports Manasseh's repentance (2 Chronicles 33:12-20). Kings focuses on Manasseh as the final straw that causes the exile, but Chronicles encourages us that even the most wicked can repent and be restored. If God restored Manasseh, then surely there is hope for the nation. At the end of the prophesied exile, Cyrus gives the decree allowing Israel to return home, leading into the books of Ezra and Nehemiah.

Living It Out

Restoration: Readers often rip 2 Chronicles 7:14 from its context (as a promise to Israel), but we would make a grave mistake to overlook it altogether. It provides the pattern for God's people to receive his blessing: humility, prayer, and repentance. James 4:10 makes the same point. If we humble ourselves before God, he will lift us up. Or as 1 John 1:8-9 declares, it is useless to deny our sin because God already knows the extent of our sinfulness, in full. But if we confess our sins, he will forgive us and cleanse us.

Temple: The books of 1 and 2 Chronicles give us a lot of detailed information about the Temple's construction, but the presence of the Lord carries forward a major theme that appears from the Pentateuch on (see Exodus: Living It Out). God's presence is lost in the Garden in Genesis, restored in Exodus, returns in the pillar of fire and then in the Tabernacle, remains in the Temple, is lost in Ezekiel, and is partially regained in Haggai. The Chronicler, with the exile fresh in his mind, neither takes the Temple for granted nor treats it as a talisman that protects people apart from a real relationship with God. Solomon's dedication prayer in 2 Chronicles 7 ripples with the knowledge that God's presence really dwells in heaven, and that no human building could ever contain him

(Hebrews 9:11). When Jesus referred to his body as "this temple," he was making an extravagant claim that *he* was the place where God dwelled (John 2:19). Incredibly, Jesus bestows on *us* the same honor, both individually and corporately (1 Corinthians 3:16-17; 2 Corinthians 6:16; Ephesians 2:20-22; 1 Peter 2:4-5; Revelation 3:12). Chronicles ought to put us in awe of God's grace in giving us access to such intimate worship. And it should motivate us to worship in spirit and in truth (John 4:22-24).

Questions for Review

1. Why are both 1 Samuel–2 Kings and 1 and 2 Chronicles necessary? What would we miss if one were left out?

2. Explain the importance of the opening genealogies.

3. How would you describe the tone of Chronicles, especially compared to Kings and the Latter Prophets?

24

Jesus in the Writings

WE SEE JESUS in the Writings by observing God's enduring faithfulness. These books take place from the time of the judges (Ruth) through the united monarchy, the division of the nation, the exile, the return, and the reconstruction. Daniel even considers the distant future—and the Lord remains faithful through all of it. He remained faithful to Job, even when Job could not understand. He remained faithful to Ruth and Naomi when wickedness had consumed Israel. He remained faithful to Esther, living in a Gentile court. He remained faithful to Nehemiah, helping him in the background even when the people did not live up to their obligations.

If God has kept all of those promises over all this time, carefully working in history despite the failures of men and women, should we expect anything less? No, the one who brought the people back to the land will send Jesus back to the earth. The one who set up David and blessed him will reign forever. The one who dwelt in the Temple will dwell in our midst and be our light. We need only to trust him in our joy *and* in our pain. He will handle the rest.

The end of Chronicles (and of the Hebrew Old Testament) echoes the beginning of Ezra. We might expect the books to be reversed, but God loves a cliff-hanger. The Law ends on the border of the land of promise, a time of joy and hope, tempered by Moses' warnings about blessings and curses. Our English Bibles end with Malachi, waiting on Elijah to prepare the way of the Lord but anxious about how the people will respond. The Hebrew canon ends with Cyrus's declaration allowing the Jews to return to their land. God has faithfully kept his promises: Will the people? When will the Son of David finally restore the nation, not as a vassal of Persia, but as a real Kingdom? The exile that Jeremiah and Ezekiel prophesied has ended; where is their new covenant? God closes out the Old Testament with so many questions.

But I have good news! Jesus is the ultimate answer.

Acknowledgments

I COULD NOT have completed this project without the support of my wonderful wife, Colleen, who remained patient with me as I wrote instead of changing diapers. She is always an encourager when I feel worn down. My wonderful children, Anastasia, Samuel, and Josiah, have been very understanding of Daddy being a little busier than usual. I am touched by their tender hearts that feel glad I am doing something for Jesus. My friends Chase Reynolds, John Strader, and Michael Hopper all provided valuable insights as missionaries with experience training pastors. I admire each of you more than words can say. Thank you for what you do for the cause of Christ. I am especially grateful for Alvin Missionary Baptist Church, where I am privileged to serve as pastor, for the people's desire to see the Kingdom of God advanced, and not just our little corner of it. My uncle and aunt, Travis and Sammi Hill, graciously allowed me to use their beach house for a week while I worked on the first draft. Eden Haneline and my mom, Roseanne Gatlin, read sections of this manuscript and gave insightful feedback. All remaining errors are, of course, mine.

About the Author

Justin Gatlin has served as senior pastor of Alvin Missionary Baptist Church in Alvin, Texas, since 2018. He oversees and teaches for an extension learning center in Alvin that is part of the Texas Baptist Institute and Seminary in Henderson, Texas. He has written VBS curriculum for Bogard Press and contributed to the Church Answers book *Sermon Starters: Outlines for Every Holiday and Occasion*. He lives in Alvin with his wife, Colleen, and their three children, Anastasia, Samuel, and Josiah.

Notes

THE LAW

1. For an accessible overview of the documentary hypothesis, consult Allen Ross and John N. Oswalt, *Cornerstone Biblical Commentary: Genesis, Exodus* (Carol Stream, IL: Tyndale, 2008).

GENESIS

1. Jeffrey Glen Jackson, ed., *New Testament Use of the Old Testament* (Bellingham, WA: Faithlife, 2015).
2. Scott Hahn, "Covenant," in *The Lexham Bible Dictionary*, ed. John D. Barry et al. (Lexham Press, 2016).

NUMBERS

1. For a discussion of the large numbers in the census, consult W. David Baker, Dale A. Brueggemann, and Eugene H. Merrill, *Cornerstone Biblical Commentary: Leviticus, Numbers, Deuteronomy* (Carol Stream, IL: Tyndale, 1996), 220.

DEUTERONOMY

1. John H. Walton, "Deuteronomy: An Exposition of the Spirit of the Law," *Grace Theological Journal* 8, no. 2 (1987).

THE FORMER PROPHETS

1. Robert D. Bergen, *1, 2 Samuel* (Nashville: Broadman & Holman, 1996), 23.

JOSHUA

1. For a survey of perspectives, see *Show Them No Mercy: Four Views on God and Canaanite Genocide* (Grand Rapids, MI: Zondervan Academic, 2003).
2. Meredith G. Kline, *The Structure of Biblical Authority,* 2nd ed. (Eugene, OR: Wipf & Stock, 1997), 163.

JUDGES

1. James M. Freeman and Harold J. Chadwick, *Manners & Customs of the Bible* (North Brunswick, NJ: Bridge-Logos, 1998), 342.
2. Barry G. Webb, *The Book of Judges,* ed. R. K. Harrison and Robert L. Hubbard Jr. (Grand Rapids, MI: Eerdmans, 2012), 329.

1 AND 2 SAMUEL

1. It is possible that the Philistines were not at war with Israel *again* but *still.* Samson had failed to defeat them in his lifetime, so the nation never experienced even the temporary rest that the other judges provided. Saul didn't either!

1 AND 2 KINGS

1. For more information on Asherah, see John Day, "Asherah (Deity)," in *The Anchor Yale Bible Dictionary,* ed. David Noel Freedman (New York: Doubleday, 1992).
2. R. T. France, *The Gospel of Matthew* (Grand Rapids, MI: Eerdmans, 2007), 329.

ISAIAH

1. Jeffrey Glen Jackson, ed., *New Testament Use of the Old Testament* (Bellingham, WA: Faithlife, 2015).
2. William Sanford LaSor, David Allan Hubbard, and Frederic William Bush, *Old Testament Survey: The Message, Form, and Background of the Old Testament,* 2nd ed. (Grand Rapids, MI: Eerdmans, 1996), 276.
3. Further arguments are given in Larry L. Walker and Elmer A. Martens, *Cornerstone Biblical Commentary: Isaiah, Jeremiah, & Lamentations,* vol. 8 (Carol Stream, IL: Tyndale, 2005), 3–5. See also John N. Oswalt, *The Book of Isaiah: Chapters 1–39* (Grand Rapids, MI: Eerdmans, 1986), 23–28.
4. Some have seen an oblique reference to Jesus in 1:3, where the word translated "care" in the NLT is literally "feeding trough." If correct, this is a sad commentary: the animals knew their Lord and the people did not.
5. For interpretations of the meaning of "virgin" here, see Oswalt, *The Book of Isaiah: Chapters 1–39,* 209–14.

EZEKIEL

1. William Sanford LaSor, David Allan Hubbard, and Frederic William Bush, *Old Testament Survey: The Message, Form, and Background of the Old Testament,* 2nd ed. (Grand Rapids, MI: Eerdmans, 1996), 358.
2. There are 38 echoes and 96 allusions, according to Jeffrey Glen Jackson, ed., *New Testament Use of the Old Testament* (Bellingham, WA: Faithlife, 2015).
3. For a defense of this view, see: Lamar Eugene Cooper, *Ezekiel,* vol. 17 (Nashville: Broadman & Holman, 1994), 264–68.
4. John Calvin and Henry Beveridge, *Institutes of the Christian Religion,* vol. 1 (Edinburgh: Calvin Translation Society, 1845), 128.

THE MINOR PROPHETS

1. Paul R. House and Eric Mitchell, *Old Testament Survey,* 2nd ed. (Nashville: B&H, 2007), 231.
2. The major arguments for this position are summarized in D. A. Garrett, "Joel, Book Of," in *Dictionary of the Old Testament: Prophets,* ed. Mark J. Boda and Gordon J. McConville (Downers Grove, IL: InterVarsity, 2012), 450–52.
3. Moisés Silva, "Galatians," in *Commentary on the New Testament Use of the Old Testament* (Grand Rapids, MI: Baker Academic, 2007), 802.
4. There is some ambiguity in how to count them. There are 19 unique verses and 22 total allusions in Jeffrey Glen Jackson, ed., *New Testament Use of the Old Testament* (Bellingham, WA: Faithlife, 2015).
5. There are 39 allusions, 16 echoes, and 4 citations according to Jackson, *New Testament Use of the Old Testament.*
6. Many authors see these as originating with two different writers. For an evaluation of that claim, see Bill T. Arnold and Bryan E. Beyer, *Encountering the Old Testament: A Christian Survey,* third edition. (Grand Rapids, MI: Baker Academic, 2015), 458.
7. Spelled *Jeshua* in the NLT, but *Joshua* in Hebrew.
8. Mark J. Boda, *The Book of Zechariah,* ed. R. K. Harrison and Robert L. Hubbard Jr. (Grand Rapids, MI: Eerdmans, 2016), 396–409.

PSALMS

1. See Mark D. Futato and George M. Schwab, *Cornerstone Biblical Commentary, Vol 7: The Book of Psalms, The Book of Proverbs* (Carol Stream, IL: Tyndale, 2009), 5–6.
2. Derek Kidner, *Psalms 1–72: An Introduction and Commentary,* vol. 15 (Downers Grove, IL: InterVarsity, 1973), 53. See also Futato and Schwab, *Cornerstone Biblical Commentary, Vol 7, 76.*

3. I am using a modified version of the classifications given in Gordon D. Fee and Douglas Stuart, *How to Read the Bible for All Its Worth,* 4th ed. (Grand Rapids, MI: Zondervan, 2014), 219–23.

4. D. Martin Lloyd-Jones, *General Considerations: A Sermon on Psalms 42:5,* https://www.mljtrust. org/sermons-online/psalms-42-5/general-consideration/.

PROVERBS

1. This section is almost certainly adapted from a much earlier Egyptian document, the Writing of Amenemope. See Michael V. Fox, "The Formation of Proverbs 22:17–23:11," *Die Welt Des Orients* 38 (2008): 22–37.

FIVE FESTAL SCROLLS

1. For an even-handed and thorough presentation of both viewpoints on the author of Ecclesiastes (that comes down in favor of Solomon), see Duane A. Garrett, *Proverbs, Ecclesiastes, Song of Songs,* vol. 14 (Nashville: Broadman & Holman, 1993), 254–64.

DANIEL

1. For an irenic assessment, see Tremper Longman III, *Daniel: NIV Application Commentary* (Grand Rapids, MI: Zondervan, 1999), 21–24.

2. Jeffrey Glen Jackson, ed., *New Testament Use of the Old Testament* (Bellingham, WA: Faithlife, 2015).

3. J. Paul Tanner, *Daniel,* ed. H. Wayne House and William D. Barrick (Bellingham, WA: Lexham Press, 2020), 250–54.

If you liked this book, you'll want to get involved in

Church Member Equip!

Do you have a desire to learn more about serving God through your local church?

Would you like to see how God can use you in new and exciting ways?

Get your church involved in Church Member Equip, an online ministry designed to prepare church leaders and church members to better serve God's mission and purpose.

Check us out at **www.ChurchMemberEquip.com**